I went to a theme p
pool table. The cue

I decided to go horse riding, something I used to love doing but had not been able to do for a few years now. It turned out to be a big mistake. I got on the horse and started out slowly, but then we went a little faster, before I knew it, we were going as fast as the horse could go. I couldn't take the pace and fell off, but caught my foot in the stirrup with the horse dragging me. It wouldn't stop. Thank goodness the shop assistant ran out of the toy shop and unplugged the machine.

Bought a second hand 40 inch plasma TV today off eBay for £5. The only thing wrong with it was that the volume control was stuck on maximum. It was an offer I couldn't turn down.

I applied for a job at the Citroen factory today. They asked for 2 cvs.

Just seen a car being driven by a sheep in a swimsuit. It was a lamb bikini.

The flat earth society are pleased to announce they have members from all around the world.

An explosion in a Burnley pie factory has caused £3.14159265359 of damage.

You know what I hate? People who answer their own questions.

Is it just me, or are there any other anagrams of em?

When I was younger, my parents used to hit me with the telephone. I was always on the receiving end.

I spent 4 hours last night making a belt out of fresh herbs. What a waste of thyme that turned out to be.

Bought a pack of extra strong mints today. Can't get them out of the packet.

Our house was burgled yesterday and all they took was an Oxford English Dictionary. I'm lost for words.

After his dog mauled my son, my neighbour came round with a piece of my sons face saying it's stained his carpet. He's got a bloody cheek.

Statistically, 6 out of 7 dwarves are not happy.

I had a spot on my shoulders - it's finally come to a head.

Some accuse me of being a luggage denier. I want to assure everyone, that is definitely not the case.

My new job as a Kwik Fit Fitter was going so well. Then the wheels started to come off.

Reports that suggest Little Miss Muffet has contracted food poisoning have been described as "Whey off".

Archaeologists have found the tomb of an ancient Egyptian ruler who was embalmed in chocolate. Apparently his name was Pharaoh Rocher.

Soon, Madagascar will have to rename itself Madahybrid.

Phoned my mum today & told her I've just opened a theatre in Bath. She said "Are you having me on?" I said I'd give her an audition, but couldn't promise anything.

There was a fat woman stood in front of the Italian section at the supermarket today.
I struggled to get pasta.

Disney are to make a movie about a Dutch boy who loses his picnic on the way to school.
It's called "The lunch-pack of Rotterdam".

50% of analysis is anal.

I've got a Dalek egg timer. After four minutes it screams "eggs terminate... eggs terminate..."

I was in an important meeting when my secretary came in to tell me I had a phone call.
"Is it urgent, Tina?" I asked. "No" she said. "It's from Huddersfield".

OK. Who's the smartass who put this "W" in my pack of M&Ms?

I can't speak for anyone else, but I think I'm a terrible ventriloquist.

I've recently changed my energy supplier. I'm now drinking relentless instead of red bull.

How does it change many dyslexics to take a light-bulb?

I can tell that my skincare puns have made you cry because of how moisturiser.

My fine art and fragrances business has failed. The perfumes sold well, but I didn't really know how to market the paintings I'd bought. I've got more Monet than scents.

I used to hate it when my mum would dress me and my brother in the same clothes.
We could hardly walk.

If anyone ever tells you they've lost their voice, they're lying.

Just had a bit of a mix up at Tesco when the cashier said 'strip down facing me'. Apparently she meant my cash card.

I had a dog named Minton who had an unfortunate habit of eating shuttlecocks. Bad Minton.

When my daughter came home from school to find her pet rabbit missing she looked everywhere for it, eventually asking me, "Where can he be?" "Maybe you should look somewhere where there might be carrots" I suggested. "That's a good idea" she replied "And peas, onion and gravy" I replied as i dished up stew for dinner.

Rap is 75% Crap

My Mum used to tell me that carrots would make me see better. Don't think so. I traded my pair of glasses for two of them and now I can't see anything.

Egg white based desserts are by far the tastiest. Am I right or a meringue?

Went Snail racing yesterday, mine kept coming last, so, to try & improve his chances, I took his shell off. Didn't work though, he was still slug-ish.

What did the slug say as he slipped down the wall?
How slime flies.

I bought a gallon of tippex yesterday, big mistake.

I met this bloke with a didgeridoo and he was playing
Dancing Queen on it. I thought, "That's Aboriginal".

When I was younger my Grandma used to rub lard
into my Grandpa's back when he was ill.
He went downhill fast after that.

I was reading a book earlier today, The History of
Glue.... I couldn't put it down.

I was in the jungle and there was this monkey with a
tin opener. I said, "You don't need a tin opener to
peel a banana". He said, "No, this is for the custard".

What do you call a chicken staring at a lettuce?
Chicken sees a salad.

I've placed a bet today that someone is going to
score a goal from 60 yards. It's a long shot, but you
never know.

My house has grass to the back, the front and to the
left of it. I want some to the right, but, as it's a semi
detached house, it seems a four lawn hope.

I was skint today and spent my last pound on a scratchcard. I couldn't believe my luck. I had nothing to scratch it off with.

I've just found a way to stop water coming into your home. Don't pay the water bill.

An Englishman, a Scotsman, an Irishman, a Welshman, a Ghurkha, a Latvian, a Turk, an Aussie, a German, a Yank, an Egyptian, a Jap, a Pakistani, a Mexican, a Spaniard, a Russian, a Pole, a Lithuanian, a Jordanian, an Armenian, a Kiwi, a Swede, a Finn, a Canadian, an Israeli, a Romanian, a Bulgarian, a Serb, a Swiss, a Greek, a Singaporean, an Italian, a Norwegian, an Argentinian, a Libyan, a Muslim, a Hindu, a Buddhist and an African went to a night club.
 The bouncer said, "Sorry, I can't let you in without a Thai".

I got run over by a limousine this morning. Took bloody ages.

I don't trust stairs, they're always up to something.

I'd find some affordable glasses, in an eye deal world.

A bloke was stealing things in Tesco at the weekend whilst balanced on the shoulders of a couple of vampires. He was charged with shoplifting on two counts.

I tried to sign up to a dyslexic website the other day. I put my password as "BeefStew" but the site said the password wasn't stroganoff.

I've hooked my mobile phone up to my TV. I'm screening all my calls.

I was really stoned today when I walked into an 'EXIT' sign. I thought, "Way out man".

To do list:
(1). Go to pet shop.
(2). Buy bird seeds.
(3). Ask how long it will take for the birds to grow
(4). Watch their reaction

I was doing some DIY, so I went to the library and asked if they had any books on shelves.

I've just left feedback for my second hand telescope I bought from eBay. Rubbish; 2 Stars.

I'm on this new diet. It's called 'I only have £10 till pay day'.

To all the people who didn't do very well in their GCSEs. No gherkin in my burger please.

I don't agree with the new law on not smoking in a car with under 18's in it. Last week my kids got soaking wet in the rain while I was having a fag in the car. They were literally banging on the windows begging me to let them in, but as I explained to them, it's illegal. Stupid law really.

Watching the Paralympics has taught me so much about acceptance of other people's different abilities but also...If they can lift more, throw further and run faster than me, how come they still get to park closer to Tesco?

Just went down the barbers in town. "How much for a haircut?" I asked "£20" he said. "That's a bit steep" I replied "How much for a shave?" "£5" he said. "Shave my head then" I said.

Just went to Lidl for some bread and came back with a two man tent, a fold up wardrobe and a generator.

My old man always used to say "Fight fire with fire"....Which is why I probably failed the fire brigade test.

An investigation has been launched after a midget was pick pocketed earlier today. Police are wondering how someone could stoop so low.

This morning I sat up in bed waiting patiently for Alfred, my butler, to bring me a big plate of bacon and eggs and a copy of the Gotham Gazette. And then I remembered, I'm not Batman.

Just bought a train ticket to Belgium & the ticket collector said "Eurostar". I said "Well I've been on the telly, but I'm no Dean Martin".

A Sergeant Major in Yorkshire is looking for people who can do cartwheels and then stand upright in a military way. Flipping attention seeker.

I can't believe a student got trapped in a clothes horse and people just laughed. Don't they realise, she could have dried.

I've joined weightwatchers. It entitles me to be weighed each month but this month I'm not going. It makes me feel like I'm wasting away.

I was playing scrabble the other day with my mate when I was left with the letters T, A, S, I, E, R, S and then I was dealt a D. This could spell disaster.

Eskimos have sixteen different words for snow. If they didn't, games of 'I spy' would be pretty naff.

I've just taken up speed reading. Last night I read 'War and Peace' in thirty seconds. I know it's only three words, but it's a start.

At the age of 65, my grandma started walking 5 miles a day. She's 92 now and we have no idea where she is.

I once met an Indian bloke in Birmingham and his name was Naan. He wasn't born there, he was bred.

I always found the white stripes to be a bit too middle of the road for me.

I recently found a round, black piece of plastic, with a hole in the middle and grooves on both sides. I picked it up and threw it. It flew for more than 300 yards. I'm sure that must have been a record.

Went for a meal last night and they asked me if I wanted a super salad. Feeling I ought to eat healthier I said "Yes please". After moments of weird looks, I realised they asked 'soup' or 'salad'.

Went in to a music shop today & the whole racking of drums came crashing down on me. I have severe percussion.

My best mate is called Tiba. Sometimes, I think he's a bit backwards.

I was in a job interview today when the manager handed me his laptop and said, "I want you to try and sell this to me". So I put it under my arm, walked out of the building and went home. Eventually he called my mobile and said, "Bring it back here right now" I said, "£100 and it's yours".

I was due to walk over a line of burning coals for charity today. But at the last minute I got cold feet.

I didn't sleep very well last night. I kept having nightmares about being chased through a big French house. I'm absolutely Chateauxed.

Just before I die, I'm going to swallow a large bag of popcorn kernels. My cremation is going to be epic.

I took my kids to the aquarium. "If you get really close to the glass maybe the whale will talk to you" I suggested to my son. "Grow up" said the woman behind the ticket booth.

Why did the chicken cross the road, roll in some mud, and then cross back again? Because he was a dirty double crosser.

Monday, Tuesday, Wednesday, Thursday, Friday, Saturday, Sunday. I've got a feeling today's going to be one of those days.

I went past the prison earlier and, as I did, I saw a rope being thrown over the wall and then, minutes later, a dwarf climb over the top and down the side. I thought to myself, "Well that's a little con descending".

An invisible man marries an invisible woman. The kids were nothing to look at either.

A blonde I know just text me asking, "What does idk stand for?" I text back saying, "I don't know" and she replied, "OMG, no-one does".

I should never have thrown that ghostly boomerang. I knew it would come back to haunt me.

They're selling Humps in Asda. Buy 2 Humps, get one Humphrey.

Two bank robbers were discussing their varied methods of operation. One asked the other, "Why have you painted one side of your getaway car yellow, and the other side blue?" "Because" he replied, "I like to hear the witnesses contradict each other".

I had a happy childhood. My Dad would put me inside a tyre and then roll me down a hill. They were Goodyears.

I've just seen some doorbells for sale at a price you can't knock.

My neighbours came home the other day to find me ripping their grass up. They soon turfed me out of their garden.

I was going to send you a joke all about different gasses but it seems the best ones argon.

No high winds or heavy rain forecast for tomorrow. The Met Office have advised everyone to make unnecessary journeys.

I came downstairs this morning to see that my curtains were drawn. All the furniture was real though.

My appalling puppetry skills have now got out of hand.

I've just read a book called 'The Broken Clock'. It's a timeless classic.

Finally. Just finished installing that bloody loft ladder. Now, Instructions on how to climb it :-
Step 1
Step 2
Step 3
Step 4
Step 5

I always wondered why pine forests smell of air fresheners.

"Daddy, why do they always put bus stops outside shops and post offices?"
"Well, sweetheart, it's so mummy and daddy have somewhere to park our nice BMW when we need to go to the shops or post office".

My friends are always saying I'm out of touch and disorganised, but wait until they see what I've planned for tonights New Year's Eve party.

I had cornflakes for breakfast again this morning. Times are tough at the moment being a chiropodist.

I must be ill, I thought I saw a sausage fly past my window, but it was actually a seabird. I think I've taken a tern for the wurst.

I stepped on a corn flake. Now I'm a cereal killer.

Two Koreans looking bemused at the greyhound track where they have been dropped off at,
"What is this place? " asked the first, "I'm not sure, I just asked the taxi driver to drop us at a fast food outlet" replied the second.

I was sat watching the TV with my dad when I asked him who Sherlocks' assistant was. "Watson". I said "Who's Sherlocks' assistant?"

Just watched an interesting documentary on television. It appears we actually knew very little about Gallileo. He was a poor boy from a poor family. And that's about it really.

I've just ordered a chicken and an egg from Amazon.......I will keep you posted.

There was a knock on my door and when I opened it a councillor was outside. She said, "Do you like tents?" "No" I replied. "Why?" "Well" she said. "We're canvassing the whole area".

I hate baking. It all starts innocently, mixing chocolate and rice krispies but before you know it, you're adding raisins and marshmallow. It's a rocky road from there.

The world's greatest mindreader died today. He was said to have inherited his gifts from his parents. Our thoughts are with his family.

A man has been stealing cans of Redbull everyday from Tesco's for the past month. I don't know how he sleeps at night!

Visited the local RSPCA yesterday, it's so tiny that you couldn't swing a cat in there.

I saw a microbiologist today. He was bigger than I thought.

I just popped down to the corner shop. Bought 4 corners.

Just popped to the paper shop, it had blown away.

After waiting in McDonalds for at least 10 minutes, a girl came over and said "Sorry about your wait". I replied "Well, you're not so skinny yourself love".

Just seen a black taxi with spots all over it. It must be an acne cab.

My job as a trainee astronomer is starting to look up.

I was walking past a castle the other day and i could hear someone shouting consecutive numbers out from its portcullis.......I suppose it was the fort that counts.

I've just been to a pet shop and asked the bloke whether I should give my dog a tin of Pedigree Chum or a bone. He said "What's the dog's name? " I said "Nic Nac Paddy Whack".

I've just written a song about a tortilla. Well it's actually more of a rap.

Someone sent me a lump of plasticine through the post. I don't know what to make of it.

I've just dropped my pet praying mantis in a pot of glue. Now it's a stick insect.

A guy who fell in to an upholstery machine is now fully recovered.

A will is a dead giveaway.

I answered the door this morning to a giant beetle. He smacked me in the mouth and started calling me names. Apparently, there's a nasty bug going round.

Russian dolls. They're so full of themselves.

A teacher taught his class about using a protractor, with varying degrees of success.

"Is a dolphin what?" asks Hitlers wife upon answering the phone.

I went to the library today and noticed it was flooded at the entrance so I had to roll my trouser legs up. I thought "Blimey, this is a turn up for the books".

Pulled a gypsy bird last night. She asked me if I wanted to go back to hers for a good time, and she wasn't kidding. I went on the dodgems, waltzers, ghost train and came home with a goldfish.

Two blondes having a chat. One said to the other "I just took a pregnancy test". The other replied "Were the questions hard?"

A teacher asks her class what their favourite letter is. A pupil puts his hand up and said "G". The teacher said "Why's that Angus?"

You can tell the sex of an ant by dropping it into a jug of water. If it sinks: girl ant. If it floats: boy ant.

As I waited for my Sunday lunch, I pondered the crossword. "Fifteen down, six letters, starting with b", I said. "To present as an honour, to gift". "Do you want gravy?" asked my wife. "Aah, bestow".

Had to sack the new cleaner today. She took over 8hrs to clean the house, then I found out she was a Slovac.

It says in the evening paper that a dog ran 31 miles to return a stick that it's master had thrown for it. Seems very far fetched to me.

I had to give a talk at work to a load of backpackers last week. They were on the edge of their seats.

Wind turbines. I'm a big fan.

Farting in the lift. Wrong on so many levels.

I went to a Bulimics party the other night. It was heaving.

I was feeling very emotional this morning. Went to the garage & I just filled up.

Tried to take a photo of the fog this morning. Mist.

I told my grandfather I'd been on a business trip to the French capital. "Oh yeah?" he said. "Did you see many of the Paris sights?" "They were all over the place, Grandpa" I said. "But you have to call them 'French people' these days".

If ever you feel like your life is meaningless and pointless, just remember, there's someone out there fitting indicators on BMWs.

I tried that thing today when you try and stop the petrol pump bang on what you want to pay. I was a bit late as it stopped at £20.03. When I went to pay the cashier, he said "I saw what you were trying to do, unlucky. Forget the extra". "Cheers mate" I replied, gave him my tenner & legged it.

Daily Mail online: 'The shorter the journey to work, the more risks drivers are willing to take'. Nonsense. I never take risks on my way to work. And I can get there before my windscreen's even defrosted.

A little paper bag was feeling unwell, so he took himself off to the doctors. "Doctor, I don't feel too good", said the little Paper bag. "Hmm, you look OK to me", said the Doctor, "But I'll do a blood test and see what that shows, come back and see me in a couple of days". The little paper bag felt no better when he got back for the results. "What's wrong with me?" asked the little paper bag. "I'm afraid you are HIV positive" said the doctor. "No, I can't be - I'm just a little bag" said the little paper bag. "Have you been having unprotected sex?" asked the doctor. "No, I can't do things like that - I'm just a little paper bag" "Well have you been sharing needles with other Intravenous drug users?" asked the doctor. "No, I can't do things like that - I'm just a little paper bag" "Perhaps you've been abroad recently and required a jab or a blood transfusion?" queried the doctor. "No, I don't have a passport - I'm just a little paper bag" "Well", said the doctor, "are you in a homosexual relationship?" "No. I told you I can't do things like that, I'm just a little paper bag" "Then there can be only one explanation", said the doctor "Your mother must have been a carrier".

Somebody just threw a bottle of omega 3 capsules at me. I only have super fish oil injuries but I'm lucky I wasn't krilled!

Went swimming. Had a wee in the deep end. Lifeguard blew his whistle so loud I nearly fell in.

Highlighter pens are the future. Mark my words.

Here's a bit of advice for you. Adv.

I used to know how to make those little fizzy sweets, but then I forgot. So I went on a refresher course.

Tin Tin realised he'd lost his sovereign ring while round a Yorkshiremans house earlier.
He rang up the host and asked him to look in the Quality Street for it, as he thought it might have dropped off while he was helping himself to a sweet. The Yorkshireman went to look for it, but couldn't find it and came back to deliver the bad news - "Tin tin tin Tin Tin".

Whenever I'm sat watching television, I always use my cat as a pillow and my dog as a footstool. I love my creature comforts.

I have a fear of speed bumps, but I'm slowly getting over it.

A man goes to a funeral and asks the vicar what the wi-fi password is. "Have some respect for your mother" the vicar replied. "Is that all in lower case?" asks the man.

"Sorry I'm late home" I said as I arrived back from work. "Some bloke had lost a £20 note in Tesco". "Were you helping him look for it?" asked my wife."No, I was standing on it".

Upon being barred from my local travel agents, I've learnt the following lesson:
Always speak slowly and comprehensibly when declaring interest in wanting to see Cape Horn.

Got an e-mail today from a bored local housewife, 43, who was looking for some hot action.
So I sent her my ironing. That'll keep her busy.

Got stopped by the Police yesterday and the officer asked me where I was between 5 and 11? I told him Primary School.

I phoned the local ramblers club today, but the bloke who answered just went on and on.

Well I'll be buggered, those bloody fools at the flipping hospital have only sodding gone and diagnosed me of having a mild case of blinking tourettes.

According to the most current magazine in my doctor's waiting room, every home will have a television by 1962.

I haven't owned a watch for I don't know how long.

I'm not saying this watch of mine is crap, but at least it's correct twice a day.

Did you hear about the fat, alcoholic transvestite – All he wanted to do was eat, drink and be Mary.

Visited DFS today and stepped inside a wardrobe. The manager came up to me and said "What do you think you are doing?" I replied "Narnia business".

Dogs are pretty tough aren't they? I've been interrogating this one for days and he still won't tell me who's a clever boy.

BBC News – Two pedestrians killed in collision. Blimey, how fast were they walking?

I see the inventor of the instant replay on television has died at the age of 81. His funeral is on at 11.30, then 12.30 and for those who missed it, 1.30.

A vicious murderer of campers and large marine life is at large. The area is no longer safe for all in tents and porpoises.

Imagine a world without cameras, I just can't picture it.

My neighbour knocked on my door at 02:30 this morning. 02:30 I ask you! Luckily for him I was still up playing my drums.

The amount of people that shout "Boo!" to their friends has risen by 85%. That's a frightening statistic.

I finally went to the doctors' this morning after years of my knees giving way whenever I'm in a slow moving queue. It's a longstanding problem.

I walked out of my front door this morning and saw 3 large holes full of water. I thought to myself well, well, well.

Whiteboards are remarkable.

Will glass coffins ever be popular? Remains to be seen.

It is claimed that a Scottish lottery winner is hoping to buy Glasgow Rangers FC. His wife says she has no idea what he would have bought if he got a fourth number up.

Knock knock.
Who's there?
Olivia.
No, I live here.

I just saw an onion ring, so I answered it.

What's the difference between red and green? Sod all apparently if you're a cyclist.

The Chav's Lord's Prayer:-
Our Father, who art in prison, even mum knows not His name, thy chavdom come, you'll read The Sun, in Exmouth which is in Devon, give us this day our welfare bread,and forgive us our ASBOs, as we happy slap those who got ASBOs against us, lead us not into employment, but deliver us free housing, for thine is the chavdom, the burberry and the Bacardi, for ever and ever. Innit

BGNA. I think that's bang out of order.

My dog can collect a stick from up to a mile away, or does that sound far fetched?

If you stand by the sea, it sounds like putting a shell to your ear.

Hedgehogs, why can't they just share the hedge?

Someone ripped the pages out of both ends of my dictionary today. It just goes from bad to worse.

If your girlfriend or wife says "If anything ever happens to me, I want you to meet someone new". Apparently 'anything' does not include getting stuck in traffic.

How lucky am I? I bought a tin of peas from the 99p store and there was over a 100 in it.

I've just opened a new shop and named it 'Toilets R Us'. It's a convenience store.

There's a nudist convention in town next week. I might go if I have nothing on.

My mobile fell into the sink this morning, now it's ringing wet.

I bought a chicken today to make sandwiches. It was useless, just kept running round the kitchen clucking.

Just managed to burn 1500 calories in 30 minutes. The pizza's ruined though.

I took down the fence in between my house and the next door neighbours and made a giant pasta strainer out of it. I thought he would like it, but he said it's a fence sieve.

I was driving to work this morning when I noticed a woman driving with her hazard lights on.
I thought to myself, "At least she's honest".

I was walking along the pavement and there was this sign that said, 'Pavement ahead closed. Please use other side'. It made me cross.

The other day, a clown held a door open for me. It was a nice jester.

Whoever invented the 'knock knock' jokes should get a no-bell prize.

A bloke took some shelves down in a shop today and started hitting me with them, so I ripped out a shop fitting and killed him. It was a massive counter attack.

I just bought a dog from the ironmongers. As soon as I got him home, he made a bolt for the door.

The new millipede I discovered is a fake, it's just a centipede. Well, according to a top counterfeit expert.

Two women called at my door and asked what bread I ate. When I said white they gave me a lecture on the benefits of brown bread for 30 minutes. I think they were Hovis Witnesses.

What has 3 legs and 4 arms? My sons pretty poor drawing of a snake.

I've just seen the new Batman shampoo in Tesco. I believe they are missing a key market by not producing a conditioner Gordon though.

I went to a really fancy restaurant called 'The Bible'. There were ten condiments on every table.

A red Indian introduced me to his wife today saying her name is 'Three horses'. I said, "That sounds interesting, what does it mean?" "Nag, nag, nag" came the reply.

Don't listen to the advice from Tesco. I asked them yesterday "How long can you keep a chicken in the freezer?". "Six months" came the reply. Well that's not true, I put one in there yesterday, and it's dead today.

Some people like the letter N, some don't. It divides opinion.

If Mary, James, Peter, Richard, David and John are all in separate vehicles, travelling at a constant speed of 60mph, in a forward direction with no obstacles, at which point is Mary likely to stamp on her brakes and cause an accident?

Saw a job advert today: '7.5 tonne HGV driver required'. They will struggle to get anybody that weight.

A bunch of random vowels and consonants got arrested last week for leaving a novel without the author's consent. They are all awaiting sentencing.

They say that 40 is the new 30. Try saying that to a speed camera.

I was out shopping with the wife earlier. A woman came out of Iceland and a box of frozen fish fell out of her bag and dropped onto the floor. I picked it up and put it into our shopping bag. The wife said "That doesn't belong to us, give it back to that lady". "No, Findus Kippers", I replied.

I wish I could find a job where I get paid to sleep. That would be my dream job.

I have to stop eating clocks, it's too time consuming.

Fell asleep at a party last night and someone put a tea bag in my mouth. Someone was taking me for a mug.

Apparently, they're not making shortbread any longer.

Fart jokes. Not to be sniffed at.

Jokes about ducks are not all they're quacked up to be.

Finding a woman sobbing that she had locked her keys in her car, a passing soldier assures her that he can help. She looks on amazed as he removes his trousers, rolls them into a tight ball and rubs them against the car door. Magically it opens. "That's so clever," the woman gasps. "How did you do it?" "Easy," replies the man. "These are my khakis".

I'm trying to find out who keeps tipping soil on my allotment. The plot thickens.

I was sitting in a restaurant when the bloke on the next table kept throwing cheese at me. I said to him "That's not very mature is it?"

Lollipop men. Now they make me cross.

I had a fling with a woman from my fencing club. It was a rather sworded affair.

I think I'm allergic to these low-energy lightbulbs. Whenever I switch one on, I can see naff all for twenty minutes.

My mum used to say "rinse your food before you eat it". Lovely woman, terrible sandwiches.

My divorce papers finally came through and it said that we had to split the house. Unfortunately, I got the outside.

I just saw a bloke driving a tractor shouting "The end is nigh". I think it was farmer Geddon.

The next person who asks me for pineapple juice, cranberry juice, lemonade & a slice of orange in the same glass is getting a punch.

The inventor of disappearing ink was found hanged in his home early this morning.
In his last message to the world he wrote, "

I hopped on a bus today. After five minutes, the driver told me to sit down.

A little boy walks in to the lounge one Sunday morning while his dad is reading the paper. "Where does poo come from?" he asks. The father, feeling a little perturbed that his 5 year old son is already asking difficult questions thinks for a moment and says "Well you know we just ate breakfast?" "Yes" answers the boy. "Well the food goes into our tummies and our bodies take out all the good stuff, and then whatever is left over comes out of our bums when we go to the loo, and that is poo". The little boy looks perplexed, and stares at him in stunned silence for a few seconds and asks "And tigger?"

It has been said that many chickens have perished in the recent floods. That's not so and such reports turn out to have been eggs saturated.

I'll never forget my first love. She took me outside and showed me her garden. She then showed me the hole at the bottom of her garden. Full of water. "Throw in a coin and make a wish." She said. So I did. I remember her well.

I didn't realise how good I was at teaching marine life until I phoned the Sea Life centre to book some tickets. My call was being recorded for training porpoises.

I've just been served by a clockwork shopkeeper. Bloody wind-up merchant.

Can you remember as kids we used to knock on peoples doors and run away? It still happens, it's called Parcelforce.

I just found out that the guy who stole my journal has died. My thoughts are with his family.

My mum has just had a stair lift installed in her house. It's driving her up the wall.

My neighbour attacked me with a power tool last night. One minute I was minding my own business, then bosch.

I once dumped a girl that was cross eyed. I thought she was seeing someone else.

My wife wanted a beach wrap so we went to the department store. The store guide by the lift showed that they were not all together but on the first, second and third floors. That's sarong on many levels.

Today someone told me my actions would have grim repercussions. I thought, "Aren't they what Death sits on?"

Found a card in a phone box last night that read, 'Phone this number if you want to have a good time'. So I did, a voice answered, "5pm, Friday".

A salesman held a gun to my head and forced me to buy blinds for my windows. Otherwise it would have been curtains for me.

If I had a pound for every time I've needed a coin for a shopping trolley.

During a recent breakdown I walked into a library, grabbed a copy of great expectations and attacked it with a pair of shears. I don't even know why I did it, but to cut a long story short...

I went to the signwriters and asked for a 6ft 'A', a 6ft 'S' and a 6ft 'K'. The bloke said he would see what he could do, but it was a big ask.

Just found a hat with over a hundred pounds in it. The bloke playing the guitar was a bit jealous that he never noticed it first. He chased me down the street.

Just had my water bill of nearly £200 drop on my mat. That's a lot. Oxfam can supply a whole African village for just £2 a month. Time to change supplier I think.

I made the mistake of asking an auctioneer the time yesterday afternoon.
"1.25. 1.25. 1.25. 1.25. 1.25. 1.25. 1.26."

My friend composes ditties about sewing machines. She's a Singer songwriter.

Conjunctivitis .com, That's a site for sore eyes.

A guy dressed up as an Orange came up talking to me in the street in a strange language.
I said "Sorry, I don't speak Mandarin".

I went to Poundstretcher today and spent 5 pounds. I came home with 5 stretchers.

I just gave away my dead car battery, free of charge.

Cocaine, horrible stuff. I love the smell of it though.

I thought I'd be a gentleman today and hold the door open for a young lady. Two minutes later she said "Will you sod off, I'm trying to have a poo".

Wish I never learned morse code. Couldn't sleep last night as the rain on the windows was telling me it was going to get me.

When in Australia, I listened to a man playing Dancing Queen on his didgeridoo. I guess he was an Abbariginal.

DFS are selling settees that float and can reach up to 10 knots. They've got a sail on.

My new year resolution is not to be late.

To the person who stole my shoes whilst I was on the bouncy castle. "Grow up".

Where can you find scenic pictures of holiday resorts? Answers on a postcard.

We've barely recovered from a global economic crisis and now all the rivers are causing flooding. I blame the banks.

I have a fear of speed bumps. I'm slowly getting over it.

All this talk of dangerous, genetically modified food tasting horrible is nonsense. I mean, just today I had a delicious leg of salmon.

Just as I was swimming I got an overwhelming taste of mint in my mouth. I thought to myself, Water Polo.

I'm heading to Greenwich tomorrow. Wondering what I should do in the Mean Time.

"This fishing tackle tastes disgusting" I said with baited breath.

I walked into a car showroom today and the salesman said, "What are you looking for?"
I said, "Because I can't afford to buy one".

I was being served my food in a fancy seafood restaurant, "What the hell is this?" I said to the waiter, confronting him angrily. "This isn't what I ordered". "Please, sir," he replied. "This is neither the time nor the place". "Yes it is", I said. "But I wanted the salmon and dill".

I had a poo on some greaseproof paper so my wife could trace my movements.

People who walk fast are beyond me.

I'm just off for a meeting with an Indian car maker. Tata.

I watched curling for a few hours today and I must say I found it very boring. Plus the women kept giving me funny looks through the hairdressers window.

Bought a Chinese takeaway last night. On the way home I head the bag rustle and when I looked across I could see a pair of eyes looking through the top of the bag. On further investigation, I noticed it was the peeking duck.

I walked in to the bosses office today and put a pear on his desk. "What's that?" asked the boss. I replied "The wife told me to grow it and then ask you for a pay rise".

I was out walking yesterday when I saw a rock that was 1760 yards long. I thought "Well, that's a milestone".

I saw this bloke chatting up a cheetah. I thought, "He's trying to pull a fast one".

'Seven' and 'eleven' both have the word "even" in them. I find that odd.

I invented a computer game called flabby birds. It never took off.

We blokes are so good to you women. My wife and I walked past a swanky new restaurant last night. "Did you smell that food, it smelt incredible?" she said. Being the nice guy I am, I thought "Sod it, I'll treat her". So we walked past it again.

The inventor of throat lozenges has died. There'll be no coffin at his funeral.

I wore a wig to Mass today. It was a blessing in disguise.

The inventor of hair colouring products has dyed.

My best friend died of heartburn the other day. I can't believe gav is gone.

I saw an Ugly Duckling in Wales last night, I said, "Oi, Get out of Towyn".

Had a job interview this week and one of the questions was 'What would you say was your greatest weakness?' "Honesty" I replied . "I don't think honesty is a weakness" the interviewer said. "I don't give a toss what you think" was my reply.

Some guy knocked on my door today and said, "I have a parcel for your next door neighbour". I said, "You've got the wrong house then mate".

Scientists have discovered an island in the South Pacific where chimpanzees have been evolving into apes. They're not sure of the cause at this stage but many are blaming Primate Change.

If I make you breakfast in bed, just say "thanks", none of this "How did you get into my house business?"

Whilst changing my grandson's nappy today, he squirted a jet right into my face. It nearly blinded me, but thank goodness I'd taken out PPI insurance.

I accidently swallowed some scrabble tiles yesterday. I'm going to the toilet now, it could spell trouble.

I just swallowed the A, E, I, O, U tiles from the scrabble game. There'll be an epic vowel movement in the morning.

"What's the quickest way to Cork?" I asked the farmer. "Are you walking or driving?" he replied. "Driving" I said. "Yes, that will be the quickest" he said.

Just been on a course and my tutor told me in front of all the class that my paper was marked incorrectly and I should have had a 'B' instead of an 'A'. I felt degraded.

A guy at work jumped off the top of our building today. It took some skill to land within the chalk lines.

If you ask me, fishing bait is worse than heroin. I only tried it once and I was hooked.

Growing up, I hated having a dad called Simon. I had to do everything he said.

Scientists are predicting a worldwide plague of bees this year. They're calling it global swarming.

A friend of mine always wanted to be run over by a steam train. When it eventually happened, he was chuffed to bits.

Lawyer "I have some good news and some bad news". Tycoon "What's the good news?"
Lawyer "Your wife invested £5000 in two pictures I believe are worth 10 million or more"
Tycoon "Brilliant. What's the bad news?" Lawyer "The pictures are of you and your secretary".

A lot of people are supposedly unhappy with Ukraine. Recently, I am too but you can't do much about the British weather.

Just got a note saying my hot beverage was ok to drink. It was a safe tea message.

People in the UK eat more bananas than monkeys. Last year they ate 96,753,211 bananas and only 6 monkeys.

I have a ninedency to understate things.

I combined all my wrist watches to make a belt. It's a complete wrist of time.

Most people called Polly prefer to shorten their name according to a Poll out today.

I watched an athlete run 150 meters in 10 seconds whilst carrying a large drum on his back. I thought, "That's going to be hard to beat".

"Beeeeeeeeep". A zebra walking past a self service checkout.

"I'm not fussed" said the worlds loneliest dog.

I walked past a lorry earlier that kept saying, "I am reversing, I am reversing." It was an articulate lorry.

I bought an old 747, took the wings off and took it out to sea. It wasn't difficult. It was plain sailing.

Thank you government for my student loan. I don't think I can ever repay you.

The furniture stall keeps calling me back. All I wanted was that one nightstand.

I got chatting to the man who works in the ticket office at my local train stop, and he told me of his dream to turn the attic into a high class gentleman's club. Personally I think he has ideas above his station.

Invisible Aeroplanes - Can't see them taking off.

I've just been reading that, by law, you have to turn your headlights on when it's raining in Sweden. And I'm thinking, "Who is going to let me know when it's raining in Sweden?"

I witnessed a burglary the other day and the police said they needed an artist's impression. So I stood in front of an easel with a paintbrush in one hand and a glass of red wine in the other, wearing a beret.

I lost my watch at a party once. Saw a guy stepping on it while sexually harassing a girl. I walked up to the dude, punched him straight on the nose. No one does that to a girl, not on my watch.

I can't believe that no one knew the extent of drug abuse in cycling. I saw about 150 of them peddling this weekend.

A dog has apparently been murdered at this years' Crufts show. Police are following all leads.

I just stole a bob-sleigh. Then made a run for it.

Picking a lock is surprisingly easy. They've got loads of them at B & Q.

I had an argument with a chav in Tesco about the last bottle of washing up liquid, so I squirted it all over him. He's now a mild green lairy thick kid.

Haven't seen the Michelin man in a while. Maybe he's re-tyred.

I've just seen an advert in my local newspaper.
ACCOUNTANT NEEDED. £35,000 - £40,000
I phoned them up and said "The answer is -£5,000".

I went in to our local library and asked them if they had any books on the Titanic.
"Oh yes, quite a few" said the librarian. "That's a shame", I said "They'll be ruined now".

I was telling this gorgeous blonde that I'd lost my wife. She gave me a big cuddle and said "It will be alright". I thought, it won't, she's bound to find me soon.

I've decided I want to start a career in Mirror Cleaning, it's just something I can see myself doing.

I went to America recently and I bought a mobile Chapel. It came with a full service history.

I'm going to the inaugural meeting of the Dodgem Car Appreciation Society later. They're expecting a bumper crowd.

The local farmer was explaining that he specialised in a specific area of agriculture. "What field?" I asked.

The official receiver came into my vintage clock and watch shop today. He said he was there to wind up my business.

I bought a trampoline but there's absolutely no bounciness to it. Plus the legs are on the wrong way round.

I couldn't believe it when I looked through the dictionary today. It turns out chicken comes first.

Midwife For Sale: Will deliver.

I wish my dog wouldn't keep running in to burning buildings and dragging people out.
It's the last time I get a rescue dog.

I answered the phone today and all I heard was sneezing. Bloody cold callers.

The last time 115 men in frocks met up to decide who was the best was Miss Thailand 2012.

I just nearly ended up in jail....forget this Monopoly lark, I'm playing scrabble from now on.

Passed my forklift test today. I am now a pro at lifting cutlery.

Beechams cold relief tablets are useless ...I've just eaten a whole packet and I'm still freezing.

Well, according to my cholesterol test I took today, I'm a pizza.

I got a 'Final Warning' letter from the bank today. Thank goodness for that. I didn't think they would ever stop bothering me.

I walked up to reception in the hotel and said, "Sorry but I forgot what room I'm in". "No problem Sir, this is called the lobby".

I've recently packed up smoking and it only took two patches to accomplish this. I stuck them both on my eyes, now I can't find my fags.

The other day a bloke offered me a go on his ice rink for 10p. I thought, "What a cheap skate."

Just saw the stroke advert on the TV. I know exactly what to do now if I see someone with their forehead on fire.

A random number keeps sending me loads of pictures advertising tinned meat. I hate spam.

According to a study, sales of irons have decreased.

I read in the news today that a kid is receiving half a million pounds worth of taxpayers money in speech therapy just because he can't pronounce his 'F' and 'th' sounds. At first I was outraged then I thought well he can't say fairer than that.

Women say men can't multi task. Well I'm writing this joke and driving at the sa

As I strolled in at lunchtime today, my boss started moaning at me. "Where the hell have you been?" "On a course" I replied. "Fair enough" he said, "How did you get on?" "Not bad" I replied "3 under par".

Ever since I swallowed a watch I've been keeping myself busy taking laxitives, eating lots of fruit and drinking prune juice. Anything to pass the time.

The two British cooks at the Vatican upset the new Pope this morning, his first day in office. All Tina Smith and Marge Brown asked was, "Does the Pope want a Full English for breakfast?" Apparently, annoyed by the Falklands situation, the new Pope was reported to have replied, quite tersely "Don't fry for me, Marge and Tina".

My clock died the other day, so I decided to conduct an autopsy. I wanted to determine the time of death.

Stuck on the A4 just going into the photocopier.

If the letters fall off your company logo - maybe it's a bad sign.

Tip for the horse racing today – Lunch-time 12/1.

Think I might have a shower. Yep, I do. It's upstairs.

I was at Heathrow airport waiting yesterday when this American started a conversation, "Who did you fly with?" I replied, "I don't know, they were all strangers".

I'm so annoyed. Woke up this morning and noticed that someone had cut off all the heads on my daffodils. I think it was a stalker.

I went trainspotting once. It was really easy. They're massive and make loads of noise.

I just got a text message saying "You're due thousands in compensation for that accident you had". Must've been that accident where I ended up with amnesia.

Woke up this morning and discovered a leak in my fish tank. Well, it was either that or a very large spring onion.

Bloke from Barnsley with piles asks chemist "Nah then lad, does tha sell arse cream?"
Chemist replies "Aye, Magnum or Cornetto?"

I can remember the first time I visited Liverpool, I found it very hard to leave. I had my car stolen.

Thought of a way to stop receiving parking tickets. Take your windscreen wipers off.

Feeling tired? There's an-app for that.

I wouldn't take the mickey out of midgets. I'm bigger than that.

This girl came up to me today and said she recognised me from vegetarian club. I was confused, I'd never met herbivore.

I tried using a colander yesterday to view the eclipse. I think I've strained my eyes.

I've lost my trousers that are too long in the leg, but I'm sure they'll turn up.

I used to think I was trapped in a woman's body. Then I was born.

For some reason I can only picture 25 letters of the alphabet in my mind. I can't begin to imagine why.

I'm currently engraving a bar chart into stone. It's hard graph.

When the local train station went up in flames I got interviewed by the local news.
"What did you see? Were people panicking?" I was asked. "I'd say there was more of a low commotion" I replied.

A man found dead in deep snow after he started walking home in severe weather was named by police today. Must have been quite upsetting for the family who had already named him.

Someone's been stealing my personal documents & trying to get money out of my bank account. The police aren't helping, they came round and took a statement.

It's 'Jamaican Hairstyle Day' at work tomorrow. I'm dreading it.

I just bought a film which had a star rating of 3.142 out of 5. It was a pi-rated dvd.

Just watched a documentary about landfill sites. What a load of rubbish.

I've worked every day for the last forty years or more, getting up at five in the morning, grafting until six at night, struggling to pay for fuel, mortgage and to put food on the table. Today, I was offered free housing, free accommodation, free cooked meals with the added bonus of not having to work for any of it. "I'll take it", I shouted to the judge.

I called the RSPCA today and said, "I've just found a suitcase in the woods containing a fox and four cubs". "That's terrible" she replied. "Are they moving?" "I'm not sure, to be honest" I said, "But that could explain the suitcase".

Ive jufst had my tsounge peircfed.

Once we were so poor, we only had a calendar to use as toilet paper. Now those days are behind me.

A man aged 98 has been admitted to a hospital with serious infections. Surely at his age, it would be far safer to admit him to a hospital with no infections.

Some people take beautiful pictures and cut them into pieces. That's a puzzle to me.

It's said that when life ends, your entire lifetime flashes before your eyes. However, for males, the last thing that's heard before life ends is, "I now pronounce you man and wife".

I've had an arm and a leg sliced off in a work accident. I've been told I'll receive severance pay.

My new stopwatch is brilliant. It can go from 0-60 in a minute.

Watched a movie last night called, 'No satellite signal is being received'. Boring is not the word.

I used to transport large amounts of shallots between Liverpool and Manchester by canal. I was an onion bargee.

I ate 4 cans of alphabet soup and just had the largest vowel movement ever.

This really fat girl came on to me in the pub the other night. She said "I'm out for a good time so I've left my other half at home". I thought, "Crikey, just how big is she?"

My thirteen year old daughter became a woman today. She spoke to me as if I was something stuck to the bottom of my shoe.

My wifes dog died today so I got her an identical one. Now she has 2 dead dogs.

"Knock knock" "Who's there?" "Doorbell repairman".

One by one, all of my best mates have started to become interested in men as well as women. So I'm just sitting here, watching the world go bi.

I entered a competition that was on the back of a bottle of Colmans condiments. The prize was a single hand glove. Not a great prize I mustard mitt.

My friend says he thinks I've put on weight. It's not my fault, I've had a lot on my plate lately.

I've only ever ordered a posh coffee once. It was an icy latted incident.

Just brought one of those tea cups that you can have a personal picture printed on.
I chose a picture of myself, it's a mug shot.

I just found out my recently dead kitten won a medal for having the best bum. This is a cat-ass-trophy.

I get so emotional when I talk about petrol. I'm filling up as we speak.

A 9 year old child disappears after using a cream that makes you look 10 years younger.

My girlfriend told me she had slept with six people before we met. I wouldn't have minded, but I was only 20 minutes late.

Watching a flea race the other day, I saw one of them actually had wings and told my mate to back it. I've just been arrested for fly tipping.

I remember the first time I saw a universal remote control, and I thought to myself. "Well this changes everything".

I asked 100 women which shampoo they preferred. Top answer was "How in the hell did you get in here?"

For anyone who's interested, I'll be signing books in Waterstones this Saturday at 09:00am until security notices and then throws me out.

I was lying in bed last night. I told her I still loved her.

I bought a jigsaw for my little nephew. Silly sod has only gone and cut two of his fingers off.

The police came to my door saying that my dog was chasing people on a bike. I said, "It can't be, my dog hasn't even got a bike".

I tried to do that riverdance yesterday, nearly drowned.

I said to the librarian yesterday, "I'm looking for a book by Shakespeare", "Which one?" she asked. "William" I replied.

It's not difficult to tell crocodiles and alligators apart. One will see you in a while whereas the other will see you later.

I tried my hand at birdwatching the other day. I was rubbish at it, just couldn't help twitching.

Mirror mirror on the wall, who should I see to get rid of my stutter?

As I walked up to the door of the newsagents today I saw that the sign said 'CLOSED'
"Oh, great" I yelled, looking directly at the man behind the counter, "Can you let me out please mate?"

Just been on Trip Advisor. They advise LSD and magic mushrooms.

Nothing embarrasses a psychic more than throwing a surprise party for them.

Some people say I have no idea how to run a court room. I'll let you be the judge.

Can't believe I've failed my maths GCSE for the 5th time now. Oh well, third time lucky.

Can't believe I need to buy an expensive license to transport my new kitten in my Vauxhall.
What a cat astra fee.

A famous german football player's partner, who has fallen on hard times and has had to take a job at the local supermarket.....poor Volk's Wag on B till.

I had to have my pet centipede put to sleep this week after he lost 98 of his limbs. The vet said he was on his last legs.

The Grim Reaper came for me last night, and I beat him off with a vacuum cleaner, talk about Dyson with death.

When I'm at the beach I prefer to sit in the shade. You seem to get a lot more space around you if you've got a lamp on your head.

I got my own back on this rude guy in the supermarket where I work by shining my scanner in his eyes. The look on his face was priceless.

A Pakistani Bloke came up to me yesterday and said "Short Back and Sides", then he said "Mohawk", and finally he spurted "Crew Cut". Turns out he only speaks in Hairdo.

I was in a womans beauty store in Saudi Arabia and decided to steal as much as I could, but I got caught before I finished. I got 50 lashes.

A cartoonist was found dead in his home. Details are sketchy.

At a recent interview, I was asked to describe myself in two words. I replied "Rubbish at maths".

A foreign lady at a market stall held two pineapples up at me yesterday and said "I give you two for one sir". It seemed like a fair swap, but unfortunately I didn't have a pineapple on me.

A friend gave me a load of cooking ingredients but no recipe. I thought "I don't know what to make of this".

Scenes of utter bewilderment took place at the Cross-Stitching evening at the local care home. I was simply trying to warn them of the dangers of sharing needles.

Every time I'm broke and need a drink I search desperately down the backs of the chairs for lost change. They hate me at DFS.

I just met someone called William Hill. What are the odds?

A mummy covered in chocolate and nuts has been discovered in Egypt. Archaeologists believe it may be Pharaoh Roche.

The school rang me today and said "Your son has been telling lies". I said, "Tell him he's very good, I haven't got any kids".

My mate invited me round to look at his goose farm and he's now blaming me because he's not getting any eggs. I only took a gander.

Two blondes were walking in the woods when they came across some tracks on the ground. The first blonde said "I am sure they are bear tracks". The other blonde replied "No, they look like rabbit tracks to me". They were still arguing about it when the train hit them.

I stayed up all night to see where the sun went. Then it dawned on me.

I did a theatrical performance last night about puns. It was a play on words.

Never bully dyslexic dwarfs. It's not big and it's not clever.

Some Chinese bloke pushed a little boat through my letterbox this morning. Turned out to be junk mail.

Newsflash: Unofficial reports are that Pop is dead. The thoughts are with Snap & Crackle at this time.

I know it's normal for towns to name places to reflect their heritage, but it makes you wonder about Manchester having Bury, Rusholme and Hyde.

I was accused of murder but I told my lawyer I was in a bookshop buying a copy of the Qu'ran for £1.50 at the time. He said that sounded like a pretty good Allah buy.

Local Police hunting the 'knitting needle nutter' who has stabbed six people in the rear in the last 48 hours, believe the attacker could be following some kind of pattern.

Statistically, 10 out of 8 people are thick as anything.

I used to deliver leaflets, 20 miles a day in all kinds of weather for the minimum wage. It was sole destroying.

I was so upset when someone built a 10ft brick wall around my house. I don't think I'll ever get over it.

Bought some 'rocket salad' today, but I won't buy it again. It went off before I got it home.

I was arrested yesterday for stealing some helium balloons. The police held me for a while and then let me go.

A teddy bear is working on a building site. He goes for a tea break and when he returns he notices his pick has been stolen. The bear is angry and reports the theft to the foreman.
The foreman grins at the bear and says "Oh, I forgot to tell you, today's the day the teddy bears have their pick nicked".

Woke up this morning to find my water bed was leaking. Then I remembered, I don't have a water bed.

William Shakespeare went in to a pub. The landlord said "Get out, your Bard".

I had a dream I was swimming in an orange ocean. It was a Fanta sea.

Next door neighbours dog pooed in our garden. My wife said "Get a shovel and throw it over the fence". I don't see what that solved as we still have dog poo on our lawn and the neighbours have my shovel.

I entered a painting sails on boats competition. I didn't win, I think it was rigged.

I went to the card shop today and asked, "Do you sell bereavement cards?" "Yes we do" replied the assistant. "Good, can I exchange this 'Get Well Soon' card for one?"

For the past year, I've been having an affair with a librarian. We've kept it quiet.

Broken pencils are pointless.

Velcro, what a rip off.

A man got ran over by a red lorry then a yellow lorry, then a red lorry and another yellow lorry. A policeman informs the family, "There's no easy way to say this".

Here's a bit of advice for you. Advi.

Had an unusual curry last night - Pelican .....tasted ok, but the bill was huge.

I saw a bloke walking down the street shouting "My name is Nuff and I'm a fairy". I thought that's fair enough.

Exit signs are on the way out.

Fitting instructions:
1) Lay on the floor
2) Shake uncontrollably

I'm looking to start up my own business, recycling discarded chewing gum. Just need help getting it off the ground.

If you say gullible slowly, it sounds like lemon.

A lorry has just spilled its load of Vicks Vapour Rub on the M6. Police say there'll be no congestion for at least 12 hours.

I was called a 'stupid reckless idiot' today. I replied with, "Don't keep me in suspense. Have I passed?"

If a woman watches a movie alone, who answers all of her questions?

Just got back from holiday and I wanted to sue the airline because they damaged my luggage. I showed the badly damaged remains to my insurance company. They said, "You don't have much of a case."

When it comes to ruining jokes with the punchline, I've been there, done that, got the tea cup.

On my recent visit to Australia, I got a full strip and cavity search at customs. I suppose it was my own fault really as when they asked if I had a criminal record, I replied that I didn't realise you still needed one.

I found a job helping a one armed typist do capital letters. It's shift work.

I got lost walking around London today until I saw a paving stone with the word 'GO' written on it. It was then I realised I was somewhere between Mayfair and Old Kent Road.

Our local vicar has just been made redundant. His services were no longer required.

Just got back from a camping holiday. Should have checked out at 10:00, but I couldn't be bothered to pack the kit up until 16:00. Police were called and they charged me with loitering within tent.

Did you know the shortest sentence is 'I am'. Does that make 'I do' the longest sentence?

I prefer white rice to brown rice. Does that make me ricist?

Everyone in our football team is raving about our top scorer Thomas Cook. Big deal I say...
It's not like he's Going Places.

You would have thought that with the standard of technology nowadays the government would replace average speed cameras with good speed cameras.

A Chinese spokesman has denied all spying allegations. He said "Why spy with our little eyes".

I've only ever had a step ladder. I never knew my real ladder.

Found a lovely pair of curtains in Ikea today, just couldn't resist swishing them apart. Don't know who was more shocked, me or the Somali woman.

Some bully said to me "I'm gonna rearrange your spine". I thought "Great, that's all I need. Another penis".

Sorry but this seems more important than the world ending update.
WARNING, PLEASE READ - If someone comes to your front door, and asks you to remove your clothes, and dance in your front yard with your arms in the air.. DO NOT do this, IT IS A SCAM!! They just want to see you naked. Please copy and post this to your status on Facebook. I wish I had received this yesterday.... I feel so stupid now.

People used to laugh at me for being too naive. They'll wish they hadn't when they find out I've won the Nigerian lottery twice in one week.

I was only young when I learned to count. It was odd at first, even then.

I took my dog to the park today and played frisbee with him. He was useless. I think I need a flatter dog.

This new digital camera I just bought says the shutter speed is so fast you can photograph a hummingbirds wings, or a woman with her mouth shut.

Trying to get through on the phone to a self-harm therapy group but I keep cutting myself off.

Sometimes I drink Coke and I'm happy, other times I'm sad. I think I'm bi-cola.

I sent off for a vault and a speaker be delivered to my house the other day. They arrived safe and sound.

A man has three budgies in a cage but had only paid for one of them, which one was it?
The budgie at the bottom of the cage because the other two were on higher perches.

My upstairs neighbour made a ground-breaking discovery last night. He can't fly.

A farmer came up to me and said, "I have 78 sheep, can you round them up for me please?" I said, "Sure can, 80".

The female praying mantis devours the male within minutes of mating, whereas human female prefers to stretch it over a life time.

There was a knock at the door this morning, so I opened it and there was a basin on the doorstep. I thought, "I'd better let this sink in".

Microwaves, for when you want a delicious piping hot bowl of cold food.

The recent US shootings remind me of the days in the UK when you could stroll into a shop and purchase a revolver. Days of a buy gun era.

I just got back from my holidays in the Ukraine, I met a chick in Kiev.

Dolphins are so smart that within a few weeks of captivity, they can train people to stand on the very edge of the pool and throw them fish.

Why did the shark cross the sea? To get to the other tide.

A man looking for work knocks on a farmers door and asks if he has any odd jobs. The farmer replies, "Yes, milk the horse".

Those scientists proclaiming grapheme to be the thinnest black material ever developed have obviously never bought Aldi value bin liners.

The girl on the bus was talking very loudly in to the mobile phone that was glued to her ear. "Excuse me," I said, "The whole of the bus doesn't want to hear your conversation." "Chill out man," she replied, "I is jus' rappin' wiv me bro innit". I felt really guilty, if I'd known she had learning difficulties, I wouldn't have mentioned it.

Light travels faster than sound. This is why some people appear bright up until you hear them speak.

Whenever I fill out any forms and they ask 'In an emergency, notify/contact'. I always put 'a doctor'.

Whilst driving down the autobahn, a car in front of me suddenly careered left in a to a sausage factory. Looks like he took a turn for the wurst.

Sewing – It's not always what it seams.

Been asked to make a reality show about fat call girls & obese criminals spending time together at a health spa. Not sure I'm going to do it yet, I need to weigh up the pros and cons.

I used to own the companies that make indigestion tablets, but they've recently dissolved.

Sometimes I love to drive off-road, across fields & through rivers. Or, 'shortest route' as the satnav calls it.

Always borrow money off a pessimist. He won't expect it back.

A bloke just came in to my pet shop and pointed at a tiny salamander and said, "That's minute". I said, "Not until you've paid for it."

Everyone is blaming me for the animal noises that were heard on the video conference at work today. Seems like I've been made the skypegoat.

It's proving very difficult to find a shop selling 'Left Guard' for my other armpit.

When they first invented the baton they didn't really like the idea, but they still ran with it.

A clear conscience is usually the sign of a bad memory.

When tempted to fight fire with fire, remember that the Fire Department usually uses water.

I hate these new parents who do all that baby talk. Yes I do, yes I do.

I was in the shop this morning and the assistant asked me what I was looking for. "So I don't bump in to things." I replied.

The recipe said, 'Put the stew in at 180 degrees', so I did. Now it's all over the bottom of the oven.

A UPS delivery driver asked me the time. I said "Somewhere between 08:00 and 18:00".

Nothing says I have total faith in God than the bullet proof glass on the Popes car.

I got stuck listening to two hipsters in a hifi shop today, arguing over amplifiers and how some digital and valve amps 'were gay'. I am sick of all these stereotypes.

I'm watching a program about reverse origami. I can't wait to see how it unfolds.

Hoodie 1: If it wasn't for our Grandads' bravery on D Day, we'd be speaking a strange language now.
Hoodie 2: Know dat true say and ting fam.

I really wish I knew who kicked the jack out from under the car I was working on. The suspension is killing me.

Anybody see that program on TV last night about Fort Knox. It was interesting, but hard to get in to.

My local Tesco has disabled parking. I'm not going back until they turn it on again.

As the dog sat watching the orchestra, he stared at the conductor and thought "Just throw the bloody thing".

I went to a cocktail bar last night and had a Cosmopolitan. I thought it was a bit dry and papery.

The police officer sat me down and said to me "Now in your own words, can you tell me what you saw?" I thought to myself "I don't have any own words, I've just been using the same words as everybody else".

I was talking to an Owl earlier and I suggested he should get on twitter. He had a good point though, 'Tweet to who?'

I've got a job answering the phone at the circus. I have to pick it up within three rings.

I got kicked out of a club last night after dropping a couple of E's. They take things very seriously at the scrabble club.

I spoiled my ballot paper. I took it for a meal and showed it a good time.

Someone just robbed me and stole my watch. I would have chased them, but I didn't have the time.

I took some advice recently and decided not to put all my eggs in a single basket. I looked a right fool walking round Tesco.

A hire van ran over my foot today. Bloody Hertz.

Decided to make use of my attic. Started to build yachts in it, sails are going through the roof.

I brought my grandson an action man for his birthday, but he told me he wanted a red Indian. Since then I've been trying to put a brave face on it.

A group of road tarmacers disappeared over the weekend, police sent out search parties but no joy. Luckily enough they resurfaced on Monday.

I met this guy who said he was a Mir space station engineer. But I thought it was quite an achievement.

Great Misheard Quotes from History - Number 12. "Watson, I deduce this must be the right bed because there is only a duvet"."No sheet Sherlock?"

I saw a man with a trolley full of horseshoes and rabbits' feet earlier, trying to get it up a hill. I thought, he's pushing his luck.

Just ate a garden hose. It was mouthwatering.

I said to my co-pilot, "What's that mountain goat in front of us doing on top of that cloud?"

No matter how much I try and buy supermarket conveyor belt dividers, the cashier keeps on putting them back.

I bought a new wig today made out of bum fluff. Bloody thing keeps blowing off.

I would like to announce that I have sex daily. Sorry, that should read I have dyslexia.

Trilby, sombrero, bowler, deerstalker, baseball cap, fez, beanie. That's a list of hats off the top of my head.

Army chief says "Cuts could be dangerous". Let's hope nobody tells him about guns and bombs.

Yesterday evening I had to change a lightbulb, a bit later on I crossed the road, then I walked into a bar. My life is just one big joke.

I've just been playing candy crush. I threw a Mars bar onto the floor at the local weightwatchers.

My mum always warned me of the dangers of glue sniffing. But I stuck to it.

Making everyone happy is impossible. Pissing them off is a piece of cake. I love cake.

Scientists who were against genetic engineering have managed to cross a seagull with a sheep, which is a massive ewe tern.

The other day I found an Action Man doll on my doorstep. That was followed the next day by a model car. This morning there was a Barbie. I think someone's toying with me.

Delays are expected on the East coast main line to London this afternoon after a swan landed on the track. Network rail say it was a cygnet failure.

I have been researching my family tree - turns out I come from a long line of ancestors.

Had a scary moment when I was opening my expensive new furniture with a Stanley knife. I damn near slit my shelf.

I tried to get on the London Eye today but it wasn't working. It was on the blink.

I fell off a 50ft ladder at work today. Luckily I was on the bottom rung.

Met an old flame today on match .com.

The bishop came to our church today. I think he was an imposter. Not once did he move diagonally.

I was delighted when the kind people at the Inland Revenue wrote to me recently, telling me that my tax return was 'outstanding', particularly since I can't even remember sending it in.

According to my sauces, I need to get out more and stop talking to my condiments.

I have an evil masterplan. I'm going to drill a huge hole through the Moon and thread a massive piece of string through it. Then I will finally be able to conker the World.

A female deer is called a 'hind'. These 'hind's' have a field of vision of about 310 degrees. A pupil about 10 times larger than ours allows them to gather in 10 times more light than us, which is why it is easy to understand why deer can run through the woods on the darkest nights without crashing into trees. Isn't hindsight a wonderful thing?

First thing this morning, there was a tap on my door. Funny sense of humour my plumber has.

I got thousands of letters delivered to my house this morning. That's the last time I order a dictionary from Ikea.

"You lied" she shouted, "You said you had between 10 and 15 million pounds in the bank".
"I didn't lie" I replied, "I have precisely £21.75".

Apparently Cadburys are bringing out a new oriental chocolate bar. It could be a chinese wispa.

"Hi honey, I'm home" I called as I came through the door this evening. I have a great relationship with the jam and marmalade as well.

I asked God for a bike, but I know he doesn't work that way, so I stole a bike and asked for forgiveness.

I asked the ticket office at the local train station today for a return ticket. The assistant asked "Where to?" I replied, "Back here".

Just been chopping up the carrots ready for dinner tonight when I noticed what looked like the Grim Reaper standing behind me. Do you think I have been dicing with death?

I fell in to the beaver enclosure at the zoo today. I'll be damned.

I went to my local Chinese takeaway. I could hear the guy behind the counter, but I could barely even see the top of his head. They must be short staffed.

My old Grandad has always tried to convince me that manure is the best thing to put on rhubarb. Forget that, I'm sticking with custard.

A chicken saw a duck standing by the side of the road. The chicken says "Don't do it pal, you'll never hear the end of it"

Apparently a lorry has spilled its load of bricks and cement all across the motorway. Police say the queues are building.

There were thousands of ugly ducklings in Rhyl today. Someone must've told them to get out of Towyn.

My pal Harry Vaderchy has been having problems making friends in Italy. He tells them his name and they just walk away.

I used to date the woman who is the voice of the speaking clock. She was so in love with me, until I cheated on her. Now she won't even give me the time of day.

I was going to get some worming tablets for my cat this morning but now I don't need to.
I looked out of the window and saw him swallowing the early bird.

Shouldn't the Air and Space museum be empty?

In Jamaica you can get a steak and kidney pie for £1.75, a chicken and mushroom pie for £1.60 and an apple pie for £1.50. In St Kitts & Nevis, a steak and kidney pie will cost you £2.00, a chicken and mushroom pie for £1.80 and an apple pie for £1.75. In Trinidad & Tobago, the steak and kidney pie is £2.50, the chicken & mushroom pie for £2.25 and the apple pie for £2.00. These are the pie rates of the Caribbean.

The canal near me stinks. It must be the onion barges.

Just bought this really rare Manx cat from some bloke down the pub, only paid £200 for it. Apparently, it's so rare because hardly any of the other cats from there have a tail.

A man said to his friend "I've just been to the dentist". His friend replied "So, does your tooth still hurt?" The bloke responds "I don't know, he kept it".

I'm making a fortune selling home security systems. The sale is easy. All I have to do is say "Hello" ....at 3 in the morning .... whilst sitting on the end of their bed.

The latest figures show crime rate in high rise flats is increasing every day. That's wrong on so many levels.

I went to the greengrocers today and I picked up an iceberg lettuce. I said to the man at the counter, "Why is it these seem to be getting smaller and smaller?" "Global warming" he replied.

Wore my new aftershave today, smells like breadcrumbs. The birds loved it.

My therapist told me that a great way to let go of your anger is to write letters to people you hate and then burn them. I did that and I feel much better but I'm wondering do I keep the letters?

A 13 year old weasel walks into a bar and approaches the bar. The bartender immediately notices the underage weasel. "Sir, you look extremely young, I can't serve you anything alcoholic" "Well what other drinks do you have?" replied the weasel. The barman replies, " Tea, coffee, juices, pop or water". "Pop" goes the weasel.

A cowboy goes into a bar and orders a whisky. He takes the gun out of the holster on his right hip and places it on the bar. "Nice gun" says the bartender, "but what are those six notches on it for?" "That's to mark the time when I killed six injuns" says the cowboy. Some time passes and the cowboy orders another whisky. He takes the gun out of the holster on his left hip and places it on the bar. "That's a nice gun too" says the bartender, "but what are those twelve notches on it for?" "That's to mark the time when I killed six Mexicans" says the cowboy. "Hold on a minute" says the bartender. "How come you get six notches for killing six injuns, but twelve notches for killing six Mexicans?" "Because" says the cowboy draining his whisky, "When you kill a Mexican, it's bonus notches".

I see yet another shop selling really big butter knives has opened up on our high street. They're becoming more widespread.

Yesterday when I came home from work, I saw a jogger running naked. I shouted, "Hey, what are you doing that for?" He shouted back, "Because you came home early".

I knocked over a tin of paint today, it got me very emulsional.

What if there was a Braille sign that said don't touch.

Was in the West End of London today, saw all the rich mothers with their babies. People were coming up to them and saying "Gucci, Gucci, Gucci".

After finding 5 Mars bars, 3 Snickers, a Flake and a packet of m&m's, I'm starting to think I'm not cut out to be a bounty hunter.

Well I learned something today, Copper Nitrate is a chemical compound, and not overtime for the police.

Special of the day in our local restaurant today was Dalas. Curious, I asked the waiter what it was. His reply was "mixed salad".

I bought a Greek yoghurt today, he said the thought was nice but could he have the cash next time.

I couldn't afford to take my kids to Sea World, so I took them to Billingsgate Fish Market, saying, "Shhhh, they're all asleep".

Lord, if you want me to be a lollipop man, give me a sign.

If you've been trying to ring me, leave me a voice mail .... someone from the News of the World will get back to you.

There's a free pool competition on at my local tonight. There's already a long cue.

If a midget smokes weed, does he get medium?

Man who wants pretty nurse, must be patient.

For a second there, I thought my watch had stopped.

I couldn't sleep last night because of clucking and squawking noises coming from the street outside. Then when I left for work this morning, there were eggs all over the pavement. Bloody hen parties.

Passionate kiss, like spider web, leads to undoing of fly.

Why is no-one ever the right amount of whelmed?

When I was a kid, my parents used to make me walk the plank. We couldn't afford a dog.

We had a delivery of a big roll of bubble wrap today. I asked my manager where he wanted it. He said "Just pop it over there in the corner". Well that passed a good 3 hours.

Lady who goes camping must beware of evil intent.

I've got a pink lighter at home. I use it for camp fires.

I've been charged with murder for killing a man with sandpaper. To be honest, I just wanted to rough him up a bit.

What has 4 letters, sometimes 9 letters, but never has 5 letters.

My son's feeling miserable. His drama group are doing a play about vegetables and he's been given the role of a carrot. He's not a pea.

Today I did that thing where you walk into a room and totally forgot what you went in for.
It was only when my leg started to get warm that I remembered.

I'm in a band called the wedding cakes. I sing.

There's a gang going through our town, systematically shoplifting clothes in size order. The police believe they're still at large.

I hate to think what Candy Crush says about me behind my back. It keeps telling me that my friends need a life.

Looking down on my son in his coffin, I thought to myself, "Why can't the Goth sleep in a bed like any normal teenager?"

I'll tell you something, I'm about to rewrite history. History.

Want to find the cheapest rate for Stand Up Comedians or Master of Ceremonies? Go to gocompere .com.

A Scouser walked into my Adult Learning Centre this morning. "Hello there" I said to him. "You need help with your reading, don't you?" "Yes, yes I do" He said. "How could you tell?" "Because the sign on the door says No Scousers".

Squirrel who runs up woman's leg will not find nuts.

I went to the opera last night. They don't like you joining in.

Shortly after takeoff on a flight from Glasgow to San Francisco, the flight attendant, in her lovely Scottish accent announced, "Ladies & Gentleman, there has been a mix up with the catering company. They have provided 300 meals, but unfortunately, there are 360 passengers on board. We apologise for their mistake, but to compensate anyone who would like to sacrifice their meal so as another person could eat, we will supply you with free unlimited drinks for the duration of the 10 hour flight". After a couple of hours came another announcement, "Ladies & Gentlemen, if anyone is hungry, we still have 300 meals available".

Just heard on the news about the luggage murders in 1997. The police are reopening the case.

A man goes to the vet and says, "Help, my birds are stuck together". "I'm sorry, I don't understand" replies the vet, "It's toucan fusing".

Did you know that the word 'emaseht' is spelt the same backwards?

I was very disappointed with what I saw in Weston Super Mare yesterday. I was on the seafront and I saw a man and woman having an almighty domestic in front of loads of kids without a care in the world. Suddenly, the women smacked the guy in the head and it all kicked off. There was a massive brawl and someone called the police. Poor copper turned up by his own and took his baton to the man, but there was still a big fight and the guy managed to snatch it off him and began assaulting the Cop and his wife. Then the crocodile snuck up and stole all the sausages.

Man who leaps off cliff jumps to conclusion.

A man goes to a zoo and the only animal there was a single dog. It was a Shitzu.

Be careful if you are thinking of getting a rescue cat. My Nan went and got one, but when she slipped and fell one day, it just sat there and did nothing.

My granddad gave me some sound advice on his death bed. "Always invest in a good set of speakers", he said.

This bloke was hanging around my canvas dwelling so much I had to call the police, they charged him with loitering within tent.

Mary had a little lamb, her husband and family were mortified.

"Polly put the kettle on,
Polly put the kettle on,
Polly put the kettle on,
We'll all have some tea".
"Look, for the last time, I can't put the kettle on, I'm a parrot".

Welsh is a language invented by someone who was rubbish at scrabble.

I'm not wearing a back brace. Oh, wait a minute. I am. I stand corrected.

I went to church this morning and saw four gravediggers carrying a coffin. When we came out of church, the gravediggers were still walking about with it. I thought 'These guys have lost the plot'.

"I'm sure we've met before" I said, offering my hand. "No we haven't" he said, "I'm Dave Javu".

Man who runs in front of car gets tired, man who runs behind car gets exhausted.

I never wanted to believe that my dad was stealing from his job as a road worker, but when I got home all the signs were there.

I'm really pleased with my vegetable patch. Haven't wanted a vegetable in weeks.

Solar powered watch free to collector. This is not a wind up.

Let's all reflect for a moment on the inventor of the mirror.

Apparently lots of dogs die in cars during the hot summer months. Personally, I don't think they should be driving at any time of year.

Man who eats many prunes get good run for money.

After all these years, I'm ready to confess. I let the dogs out.

The bell on my bike has fell off, so I've attached a peashooter to warn people when I'm near.
I've decided to call it my no bell pea surprise.

This lunchtime, I saw a blonde spend a good five minutes trying to stab her fork into a pickled onion, with no success. "Oh for goodness sake" I snapped, sick of watching her struggle. "Just use your bloody fingers" "Don't be an idiot" she said. "They're no bloody sharper".

War does not determine who is right, it determines who is left.

War does not determine who is right, war determines who writes the history.

After years of study I can finally use the letters BSc at the end of my name. I'm that proud of my bronze swimming certificate.

I gave an elderly rabbit a Viagra but it died. I guess old rabbits die hard.

I went to a shop today and the sign on the door handle read, 'SHOVE.' I thought, "So, Push has come to Shove has it."

Saw an RAC Patrolman getting in his van today. He was waving his arms about frantically and crying his eyes out. I thought, "He's heading for a breakdown".

The man who founded ParcelForce has recently died. His funeral will be next Friday between 07:00am and 10:00pm.

I saw a sign in a shop window that read "Sal". I thought, "They've got a sale with 25% off".

I was once addicted to the hokey cokey, but then I turned myself around.

A new company called Miserable gets quoted on the Stock Exchange today. It started as a little concern and since then it's groan and groan.

Message to the bloke in the wheelchair who stole my camouflage coat in the pub last night "You can hide, but you can't run".

Just watched a documentary about people walking on hot coal. It was sole destroying.

What do you call a magicians' dog? A Labracadabrador.

Despite buying my grandson the necessary stationery, he still can't draw straight lines. He breaks all the rules.

Went to a school play Friday evening when a little boy fell through a large crack in the floor. I said to his mother "Don't worry, it's just a stage he's going through".

My boss called me. "Why are you late?" he asked angrily. "I'm stuck behind a group of bikers" I replied. "Can't you just ask them to move over?" he said. "But they look aggressive" I said, "And the barman hasn't served them yet".

My new business selling choux pastry didn't work out. It just wasn't very profiteroleble.

"My husband saved for ages to send me on this cruise" says one woman to the other "Oh, I've been on lots of cruises" says the other "Mind you, he does work for Cunard". The first lady looks shocked "Well mine works really hard too, but there's no need to swear".

I've just seen the headline 'suicide bomber strikes again'. He can't be very good can he?

Don't you just hate it when people answer their own questions? I do

I've just finished painting stripes on our little pet rodent. Its not much, but It makes the degu faster.

I've finished my first novel today. I'm so proud, I might read another.

A British company is developing computer chips that store music in women's breast implants. A company spokesperson declares this a major breakthrough, as women are always complaining about men staring at their breasts without listening to them.

A piece of black tarmac walks in to a bar and shouts out "Who wants a fight? Come on, I'll take anyone on". Nobody replied so he bought a drink and sat down. A few minutes later a piece of red tarmac walks in and shouts out the same thing. Nobody answers so the piece of red tarmac drinks up quickly and leaves. A drinker went across to the black piece of tarmac and asks why he didn't take him on. The black piece of tarmac replies, "You must be joking, he's a cycle path".

I had to bin my Hornby model railway set last night as it broke. I was absolutely gutted and upset. Everyone at work agreed though and were very supportive when I told them about it.
"Oh my god, that is so sad" they said.

I went into a bar and there was a guy at the piano playing chopsticks. He wasn't a patch on my uncle Fred playing the spoons though.

When I was young my grandad said to me "SELFISH", so I became a Fish Monger.

There's an advert in my local paper selling burial plots. I thought that will be the last thing I need.

I've just got a job at a factory making loudhailers. It's nothing to shout about.

An Englishman has started his own business in Afghanistan. He is making land mines that look like prayer mats. It's doing well. Prophets are going through the roof.

The Greek government has announced that it is ceasing all production of taramasalata and humous in an attempt to stop a double dip (recession).

Just brought a spooky boomerang. I bet it comes back & haunts me.

I recently learned how to speak Apache. It's easy when you know how.

It takes many nails to build a crib, but one screw to fill it.

I've been diagnosed with a fear of Giants – Feefiphobia.

A man was savagely attacked at the Teddy Bears Picnic yesterday. His condition is improving but he's not out of the woods yet.

The van I'm driving to deliver edible kernels keeps breaking down. It's driving me nuts.

I had the plumber round for a quote to fix my boiler. "I currently charge 45 pounds an hour" he said "I can fix it now or you'll have to wait two weeks before I'm free". "Ok" I said "I'll ring you in a couple of weeks". It's worth waiting 2 weeks if he's going to do it for free.

My fruit and vegetable business has gone into liquidation. I now sell smoothies.

Do you know who makes me cross? The Lollipop Lady.

I'm selling a limited edition bottle of Tippex. It's a correctors item.

I've just read a novel written on fly paper. I just couldn't put it down.

Some say all Chinese look the same, well I disagree. My special fried rice looks nothing like my prawn toast

I visited a Mandarin Library yesterday. It was full of Chinese whispers.

I phoned the Weak Bladder Helpline today about my problem. It's 1p a minute.

My great granddad broke his toe riding his bike. My granddad broke his arm trying to get it off him. My dad broke his leg when the bike then struck him. It's a vicious cycle.

A bloke who couldn't see, hear, taste, feel or smell hit me in the face yesterday.
I said that there was no place for senseless violence.

If Decs' Geordie friend wants to run away and get married, Africa is the perfect place for an Ant elope.

Two artists I know have finally divorced. It was a long, drawn out affair.

I wish these two tailors would get on with their fight. They've been sizing each other up for hours.

A man goes into a library and asks for a book on suicide. The librarian says, "Get lost, you won't bring it back."

Two parrots sitting on a perch. One said to the other "Can you smell fish?"

Asian guy just moved in next door. He's travelled the world, swum with sharks, wrestled bears and climbed all the highest mountains. Nice chap, his name is Bindair Dundat.

I did some shopping in Tesco last night and the checkout girl asked if I had a Clubcard. I said "I believe I do" and handed her the ace of clubs.

This bloke came up to the counter today and ordered burger and chips. I asked if he was eating in or taking out. He gave me a right mouthful of abuse. I love working in the prison canteen.

We used to have a teacher called Miss Turtle at school. Strange looking woman, but she tortoise well.

Our local postman just asked the girl across the road to marry him. He was going to ask my daughter, but he went to the wrong address.

I have just been sacked from my job as a redcoat, apparently I was treating the place like a holiday camp.

Can fat people go skinny-dipping?

Was really looking forward to my birthday, but the only present I got from my parents was some rollerblades from Poundland. "Bloody cheapskates".

I've designed a plane made entirely from rubber, so that when it crashes, it bounces. It's a Boing 747.

Tragic news from the Nestle factory today as a worker was crushed to death when a load of chocolate bars fell on him. He tried in vain to get help but every time he shouted "The Milky Bars are on me" his fellow factory workers just cheered.

Got a job today with the City Council Recreational Parks Department repairing all the see-saws. I suppose the job has its ups and downs.

Adverts - If you're so much better than the leading brand, why aren't you the leading brand?

One of my friends said to me "What kind of person would want to own a circus?" I replied "I don't know, some clown".

BBC NEWS : Fighter jet escorts passenger plane into Manchester airport after pilot reports "possible device on board". The man arrested at Manchester Airport today following a hoax bomb threat was carrying nothing more than Benylin Mucus Cough medicine said a spokesman for Catarrh Airways.

My daughter has taken up show jumping and is really very good at it. In fact, I can't fault her.

If you get an email telling you that you can catch Swine Flu from tins of ham then delete it. It's Spam.

Just spent ages waxing the car. Still can't believe how hairy it gets.

A bloke went in to a pet shop and paid £50 for a large hamster. After the first night, he woke to find the hamster had died. Having paid a lot of money for it, the bloke took it back to the pet shop and asked the owner what he was going to do about it. The owner replied, "I'm very sorry, we don't have any more hamsters left, the only thing I can suggest is to make jam from it. It's quite large so you should make quite a few jars and recoup the money you paid for it". So the bloke took it back home and made lots of jam. Just before going to bed, he sampled it, and it tasted awful. With no further ado, he threw the whole lot out in to the back garden. The next morning, when he woke up & pulled back the curtains, he saw a great big bunch of daffodils where the jam had landed the night before. Bemused, he went back to the pet shop and related his story to him. The owner replied, "Indeed, that is strange because usually you get tulips from hamster jam".

Bad quiz night. The Quiz Master asked us to name Bond villains. He just wouldn't take No for an answer.

A friend of mine has contracted a deadly disease from eating some cereal. All he had was Ebola Cornflakes.

Never employ someone who's obsessed with graphs. They'll always be plotting behind your back.

Somebody asked me how my brother-in-law died. I replied that he was a karate expert, then joined the army. The first time he saluted, he killed himself.

My son suggested I register to be an organ donor. There's a boy after my own heart.

This is a story which is perfectly logical to all males :- A wife asks her husband "Could you please go shopping for me and buy one carton of milk, and if they have eggs, get 6". A short time later the husband comes back with 6 cartons of milk. The wife asks him, "Why the hell did you buy 6 cartons of milk?" He replied, "They had eggs".

The family wheeled Grandma out on the lawn, in her wheelchair, where the activities for her 100th birthday were taking place. Grandma couldn't speak very well, but she would write notes when she needed to communicate. After a short time out on the lawn, Grandma started leaning off to the right, so some family members grabbed her, straightened her up, and stuffed pillows on her right side. A short time later, she started leaning off to her left, so again the family grabbed her and stuffed pillows on her left side. Soon she started leaning forward, so the family members again grabbed her, and then tied a pillowcase around her waist to hold her up. A nephew who arrived late came up to Grandma and said "Hi Grandma, you're looking good. How are they treating you?" Grandma took out her little notepad and slowly wrote a note to the nephew 'They won't even let me fart'.

I saw this guy walking down the road with a sign saying "& Emergency". I asked him where he got it from and he replied that he found it by accident.

I've started writing poetry. I've just got the R and the Y left to do.

A Chinaman starts working at Staples and the manager tells him to go to the storage shed and get supplies.....a week later the manager walks back to the storage shed and the Chinaman jumps out from a corner and yells "Supplies".

I went out to watch the meteor shower last night. At one end of the street was a banana split with gravy and at the other end was a bowl of custard with sausages. I thought to myself 'these streets are strangely desserted'.

Today marks the anniversary of the great train robbery. To celebrate I went into London Kings Cross and paid £4.50 for a cup of tea.

My daughter asked me to wind the baby. I thought that was a bit too much, so I gave it a dead leg instead.

Construction work has started on the new eye surgery clinic. It's a site for sore eyes.

I was sailing on a Junk in Thailand when I first met my girlfriend. I remember at the time I changed my Facebook status to: In a Real Asian Ship.

I got so excited the first time I was in a limousine that I got a little bit giddy and started mooning out of the window. I got in serious trouble. I was told I was upsetting the other mourners.

A newly wed couple on their honeymoon night are in the bedroom getting undressed when she says "Darling, now that we are married, I have a little confession to make. I was a hooker before we met. Are you ok with that?" He replies, "Of course I am, that was before we met, and to be honest, it turns me on a bit. Tell me more". She said, "Well, my name used to be Brian and I played for St Helens".

Just seen a llama at the back of Tescos. I think it's the deli llama.

I walked into a pet shop and said to the assistant "The bottom of my face is very hot".
"And what do you want me to do about it?" came the sarcastic reply. "Well, the sign in the window says you have Chinchillas for sale".

In Cairo, heavy duty vehicles driven by Government loyalists, crush dozens of tent-dwellers to death. The Egyptian curse of two ton car men strikes again.

I'm sure there's a bouncy castle in our local mosque. Everytime I go by, there's a load of shoes outside.

A cop with a drug sniffing dog came up to me and said, "This dog tells me you're on drugs". "I'm on drugs?" I said, "You're the one talking to a dog".

Bought a packet of balloons today for my grandsons birthday – £10, I suppose that's inflation for you.

Sometimes I get so angry I just want to go out and do judo moves on fat people. But there is no point throwing a wobbly.

I couldn't believe it when my son came home today with two armchairs and a settee. I keep telling him he should never accept suites from strangers.

My mate's got a new business idea that guarantees punters. He's bought a punt.

I had a man at my door today, spouting off about the sins of dirty carpets and asking if I'd heard the word of the Almighty Vacuum Cleaner. I told him to bugger off, and slammed the door in his face. Bloody Jehoovers Witnesses.

Sometimes I like to go to the hardware store and run around with a screwdriver shouting,
"Ladies and gentlemen, this is not a drill".

"It's going to be one of those days", I thought, as I stared at the calendar.

Someone asked for my religious views last week. I said that I could just about see our local church from the bedroom window.

Y G O L O H C Y S P
Reverse Psychology

A local muslim gardener was planning terrorist attacks by radio signal from his allotment, so I covered the whole area in silver paper to block the transmissions. That's foiled his plot.

A book just fell on my head. I've only got my shelf to blame.

I was chatting to someone today about cylindrical fasteners. It was a riveting conversation.

I'm off to a fancy dress party this weekend disguised as a Tupperware box. I'm so excited, I can hardly contain myself.

I've got an injured extraterrestrial in my shed. He's missing an eye.......I've called him Alen.

For a while Houdini used trap doors in every act. It was a stage he was going through.

For my next trick, I will eat a percussion instrument in a bap. Drum roll please.

Got shouted at today on a training course when I was told there's no "I" in team. Told him "But there are 5 in individual brilliance". That shut him up.

I entered a weed rolling competition today. Came joint first.

My little cousin has been diagnosed with an unusual case of OCD where all he does all day is organise dinner plates by the year they were made, it's an extremely rare dish-order.

I just bought a top of the range Rolls Royce car, but my budget didn't cover for a driver. So I spent all that money and I've nothing to chauffeur it.

At first I thought I could handle being a police detective even though I have schizophrenia, but now I'm beginning to question myself.

Even though I've gone bald many years ago, I still keep the comb I've had for over 30 years. I just can't part with it anymore.

When the giant cannibals began to soak me in vinegar, I thought "enough is enough". "Why don't you pickle someone your own size?" I shouted at them.

I read a history book about WWII that was only six pages long. It was abridged too far.

I named my dog Fetch. The poor thing doesn't know whether he's coming or going.

I just phoned our local MotherCare. They told me I have to look after my own mother.

A cowboy walked into a saloon bar with a coconut-filled chocolate bar on his head. "What's up with him?" the barman asks one of the regulars. "Oh, he's got a bounty on his head".

I've been offered a job with the noise abatement society. I don't think I can turn it down.

I recently auditioned for the main part in a new musical about Cuba. I got a call back saying they want me to be the understudy. I had to turn it down. I refuse to play second Fidel.

I had to take a palm tree back to the shop today. It was out of dates.

I'm in a band called The Mutes. You've probably never heard us.

I used to be in a band called The Leftovers. We've gone to the dogs.

Two scientists have just got married after falling in love whilst they worked on a study to discover what caused the fires of hell. Apparently it was a match made in heaven.

I don't believe in reincarnation. What's the use of coming back as a tin of condensed milk?

I'm an international spy and I travel the world carrying out missions for the British government, however, I always tell the people I meet that I work in a duvet factory. It's my cover story.

Did you hear about the poet who had Alzheimer's? He was a poet and he didn't know it.

I grew up in a really rough area. When I was a kid, people used to cover me in chocolate and cream and put a cherry on my head. Life was tough in the gateau.

My friend was scheduled for a cardiac transplant. Then he had a change of heart.

I thought chiropractors were a waste of money, but I stand corrected.

I once dated a magazine collector. She had issues.

Say what you want about my forehead wrinkles, they're making headlines.

Went in to Coffee #1 today and two customers spilt their chocolate coffee drinks over me.
Someone's put the mochas on me today.

A man who took an Airline company to court after his luggage went missing has lost his case.

R.I.P boiling water, you will be mist.

I met a fat girl the other night and she said "Hi, I'm Anita". I looked at her and said "You certainly are".

I've managed to build a car without a reverse gear or a steering wheel. It's pretty straight forward really.

I built a car that was made totally out of wood....... wooden framework, wooden chassis, wooden wheels. Went to start it this morning, wooden go.

After a talking sheepdog gets all the sheep in to the pen, he reports back to the farmer, "All 40 sheep in the pen". The farmer replies, "But I only have 39". "I know" says the sheepdog, "But I rounded them up".

I'm not sure if my ceiling is the best I've ever had, but it's certainly up there.

I just bought a film with 3.142 stars out of 5. It was a pi rated DVD.

I lost a very good friend and drinking partner last weekend. He got his finger caught in a wedding ring.

My paper manufacturing business has folded seven times, so I'm pretty sure it won't happen again.

There was a lovely mirror behind the counter at my local shop. I could see myself buying it.

I once made a profit selling my mate an old cheap metal, Turkish copy of a German car.
It was a con Stan tin Opel.

Losing all my fingers, except my middle one, has stopped me from getting where I want.
I've been hitch hiking for hours.

My local cemetery has raised its burial cost, and blamed it on the cost of living.

I work as a car mechanic and one day a Ford Fiesta rear-ended a Ford Sierra. Both cars were bought to our garage and written off. Since the back of the Fiesta and front of the Sierra were still OK, I wondered whether I could salvage anything. I got my cutting and welding equipment, spliced the two good halves together and by the middle of the afternoon I had a Siesta. It had been a pretty tiring day.

In a restaurant, I was hit on the back of my head with a Prawn Cocktail. I looked behind & this bloke shouts "That's just for starters".

Was in the Indian restaurant last night when the waiter came over and said "Curry OK?"
I said "Go on then, just one song then bugger off".

50 years on I've just been back to the church I used to go in when I was a child. I won't be going again. Everything's altared.

I passed my forklift test today. I'm now a pro at lifting cutlery.

A man got run over by a red lorry then a yellow lorry, then a red lorry and another yellow lorry. The police informed the family, "There's no easy way to say this".

A man was arrested yesterday after falling into a combine harvester whilst trying to steal it. He's due to be bailed tomorrow.

A guy nicked my garden gate. I didn't chase him off in case he took offence.

The next time you hear the annoying sounds of jack hammers and diggers outside your house, don't be so quick to think "What a bloody racket they are making out there". You don't know what good they may doing. For all you know their work could be groundbreaking.

This morning I watched the breakfast news. There were no new ideas about what to eat for my first meal of the day.

Don't you just hate that situation when you're picking up your bags at the airport, and everyone's luggage is better than yours. A real worst case scenario.

My kids keep making fun about my dementia, well they won't find it so funny when they wake up Christmas morning with no eggs under the bonfire.

I'm reading a great book about toilet seats. I can't put it down.

Did you hear what happened when the decorator painted his wife with cheese? He double Gloucester.

It's hard to say what my sister does, working for a travel agency. She sells Seychelles overseas tours.

The Inventor of the jug died today. Tributes have been pouring in.

As I was driving, I saw a bloke walk to the other side of the road and draw a large X on another bloke's face. I thought, "There's a pedestrian crossing a head".

Just bought a really basic pair of shears. They're not cutting hedge anyway.

For the last two weeks I've noticed graffiti all over my windows every morning. I have now realized it's the night drawing in.

I recently got the sack from working on the dodgems and waltzers. I'm suing my ex employers for fun fair dismissal.

A pirate goes to the doctor, worried the moles on his back are cancerous. "It's ok" says the Doctor "They're benign". "Count 'em again Doc" says the pirate. "I reckon there be at least ten".

Police have issued an appeal after receiving complaints from farmers that their cows are being stolen during the night. Apparently they are looking for a man with a big moo-stash.

Went to weight watchers the other night, dropped a bag of malteesers all over the floor, best game of hungry hippos I've ever seen.

I got talking to a woman in a hotel bar when she whispered, "Meet me in my room this evening, I'm 8e". "Really? What's your secret?" I gasped, "You don't look a day over 40".

What anti-perspirant do pessimistic people use? Not sure.

Just bought a copy of the What Car magazine. Apparently it's not full of photos of people being run over.

Just had to sack my odd-job man. Left him a list of eight jobs I needed doing and he only did jobs one, three, five and seven.

When I overheard my neighbour calling me names, I went round his house and punched his lights out. I'm regretting it now, for the last 3 hours I've been picking glass out of my hands.

I would like to thank my legs for supporting me, my arms for being by my side and lastly my fingers because I can always count on them.

I don't know why people keep getting worked up about immigration. All my neighbours are English. All the kids in the local school are English. All the local shops are owned and run by English people. I love it here in Spain.

My toughest ever job was a rep selling doors. Every time I knocked at a persons home, I thought "This is going to be hard, they already have one".

A man has been seen acting suspiciously near a bird enclosure at the local convent. Obviously a nun's aviary character.

After 30 years of marriage, I am delighted to announce I have finally lost my hearing.

Brought myself an invisible dog today. Named it Spot (the dog).

Went to a Sea-Food Disco last night, managed to pull a mussel.

I've got a dog with no legs called Woodbine, each day I take it out for a drag.

For a prank at work, some guys poured a dish of pasta over my head. I was disappointed because most of them were sensible people, it's just a shame about the fusilli ones.

Just been to buy some camouflage trousers but I couldn't find any.

Two blondes walk into a building. You'd have thought at least one of them would have seen it.

Two blokes dressed in armour go up to the hotel receptionist and request a room for two knights.

I was once abducted by aliens. They made me blow my nose, eat my greens and wipe my face. I think I was onboard the mothership.

I used to be a member of a secret cooking society. They kicked me out for spilling the beans.

I love Chinese food as much as the next guy, but you'll never convince me a chicken fried this rice.

When I sleep with the window open, I sometimes hear a woman screaming and moaning with pleasure. I wonder who the heck delivers shoes at one in the morning?

I walked into an opticians. I said, "Hello sir, I think I need some new glasses". She said, "I think you're right".

I was woken early by a couple of coppers knocking on my door. They said "There's been a serious crime and we are just looking for leads". I replied "Your way off, this is Bristol, Leeds is near Bradford".

I've just made it past the preliminary rounds of the World Hairdressing Championship. Now I've just got to plait cool.

Had to fire my tailor. It was nothing personal, he just didn't seam right.

I'm not the kind of guy to distance himself from anything. Far from it.

Is there anything more pointless than an autobiography having an 'About the Author' section?

I was chatting with my mate Dave the other day. He said, "Have you heard they're filming the new series of I'm a Celebrity Get Me Out of Here! in the West Indies?""Antigua?" I asked. "No but Decs' keen" he replied.

Miss Preston had to drop out of the Miss U.K. Beauty Pageant after she was charged with identity theft. It turns out her last name isn't even Preston.

I was on a Ryanair flight last week. The Stewardess came over and said "Tea or Coffee Sir?" I replied "I give up, what is it?"

I was selling my python and someone rang to enquire."Is it big?" he asked. "Massive" I said. "How many feet?" he continued."None" I replied, "It's a snake".

Just been on eBay looking for cigarette lighters. I got 15,000 matches.

Went on a date with a girl from the stock exchange. I knew it was going well when she started to play FTSE under the table.

I saw a fire blanket earlier. Then I thought, "That's pointless, fires are warm enough as it is".

My band is called 'The McNuggets'. We used to be called 'The Chickens' but we're recently re-formed.

I just put salt on my mobile, now it's a saxophone.

Woke up this morning and forgot which side the sun rises from. Then it dawned on me.

My mate Sid was a victim of ID theft. He's just called S now.

Jousting? Said the Brummie to the Bee.

The boss of Dulux paints has died of hypothermia while trekking across the Antarctic.
Medics say he needed a second coat.

I was about to make a joke about a short sighted stag, but I realised it was a bad idea.

I saw a guy and a girl experimenting with Methamphetamine on the side of the road.
They were speed dating.

I've spent the last few months stealing training wheels from kids bikes in the Middle East.
Thus further destabilising the area.

On the train, last night, I was kind of crushed up against a nice chick when she turned around and shouted, "Get away from me, you weirdo". Had there been anybody else in that carriage, I would have asked for their opinion.

What have Kermit the Frog and Henry the VIII have in common? They both have the same middle name.

As UK surgeons prepare to start performing full womb transplants, the Conservatives are preparing their next tax initiative with the 'spare-womb' tax.

Exit signs are on the way out.

I don't tend to tell dad jokes, but when I do, he laughs.

Imagine if the whole world decided to convert from pounds and stones to kilograms, it would be mass confusion.

Went to the tuck shop today, now my shirt is neatly inside my trousers again.

I'm feeling a little down in the mouth this morning, must have been that duck I ate last night.

Some Americans are so anti Trump they think he should be buried in concrete. Others are saying it would set a bad president.

I'm leaving all my money to a plastic surgery charity. I expect it will raise a few eyebrows.

I was in a band called cancelled. Nobody ever came to see us.

My daughter wants to quit as a ballerina but I won't let her. I like to keep her on her toes.

I've just started a band called 999 megabytes. We haven't done a gig yet.

As I sat at the table last night looking at my G & T, WKD & JD I thought, "I hate this game of scrabble".

A man asks the librarian, "Have you any books on shelves?" "Yes, all of them", he replied.

Did you know that in Bahrain they do not show the cartoon 'The Flintstones', but Abu Dhabi do.

Did you know, if you stare at a piece of raw chicken, it will eventually start to smell?

Congratulations to To Youyou winning the nobel prize in medicine and for being the most confusing person to sing happy birthday to.

Councils are saying they are losing £30 million a year in unpaid parking fines. If they halve the cost of the fine, then they'll only be losing £15 million.

I read that 111 people a week are bitten by dogs leading to 999 calls for emergency treatment. Why are they phoning 9 times?

Last night I was very proud when I ordered my over-cooked steak. Even the waiter said "Well done".

Thousands of eggs have been stolen from a farm. Police suspect poachers are to blame.

It was a big mistake I made when I dared to be different. I've never been the same since.

Did you hear about the Dutchman who had shoes made of bubble-wrap? Popped his clogs.

Think I may have a shower. Just checked, yes I do, it's upstairs.

I used to be afraid of chestnuts, but I've now conkered my fear.

I was in Tesco tonight when this woman dropped down dead in front of me. She'd just bought a bag for life. Irony's a bitch.

I bumped into the guy that invented the globe. It's a small world.

Bought a book on the history of flour the other day. Just sifting through it now.

I've had an awful day. First of all I got punched by a medieval poet, and then later I slipped up on a sausage. Things have just gone from bard to wurst.

I met the godfather of the Scottish mafia yesterday. He made me an offer I couldn't understand.

I've just got a new job in a Bowling Alley. People are asking me "TenPin", but i said "No, permanent".

Does anyone know if the arachnophobia helpline has a website?

What do you call a joke with no punchline?

I told my butler a joke about firing him because the doorbell rang all day. He didn't get it.

Been Invited to attend a lecture on the subject of quantum mathematics.To be honest, I am only going along to make the numbers up.

I'm addicted to seaweed. I must seek kelp.

Had a weird dream last night in which the Queen bestowed a knighthood on a fish.
Sir eel.

Two Chinese tourists were on a road trip. Sat Nav says 'right turn in 100m' 'right turn in 50m' 'turn right now' but the Chinese tourists continue going straight. Moral of the story - two Wongs don't make a right.

Once you've seen one shopping centre, you've seen a mall.

I saved a fortune on car insurance yesterday. I left the scene of the accident.

Went to the butchers yesterday and I bet him 50 quid that he couldn't reach the meat off the top shelf. He said, "No, the steaks are too high".

Between the Stone Age and the Bronze Age was the Copper Age. Back then, people really knew how to conduct themselves.

Just had to sack our Eastern European cleaner. She was a slow vac.

I have no objection to people being spontaneous, I just think there is a time and a place for it.

I keep on having a recurring dream of 10 ten divided by three.

I can hear music coming out of my printer. I think the paper's jammin' again.

I walked in on a guy stealing money from peoples bank cards online. He looked at me worried, but I told him "Don't stop on my account".

Fell asleep at a party last night and somebody put a teabag in my mouth. I went mental. Nobody treats me like a mug.

I see there's a new chain of coffee shops opening up in Russia. They're called Tsarbucks.

I did some odd jobs round the house today. I vacuumed the ceiling and painted the oven.

Whoever coined the phrase 'cleanliness is next to godliness' was talking out of his backside. I looked them up in the dictionary last night. Godly and godsend are next to godliness. Cleanliness was 343 pages away.

I went bobsleighing the other day. Killed 25 Bobs.

A man was savagely attacked the other day at the Teddy Bears Picnic. His condition is improving, but he's not out of the woods yet.

I woke up at 3 am and saw a scary black horse at the end of my bed. It was a night mare.

Forty gypsies from Dale Farm arrive at the Pearly Gates in their transit vans and caravans.
St Peter goes into the gatehouse and phones up God saying "I've got 40 travellers here. Can I let them in?" God replies "We are over our quota on Pikeys. Go back out to the Pearly Gates and tell them to choose which are the 12 most worthy, and I'll let just that dozen in". Less than a minute later St Peter is on the phone to God again. "They've gone", he tells God. "What?'" says God, "All 40 of them?" "No, the Pearly Gates"

Anyone who says onions are the only vegetable that make you cry has never been hit in the face with a turnip.

I've just been attacked by someone with a power tool. I was walking along the road, when suddenly, bosch.

I've got a lighter with a pink flame. I use it for starting camp fires.

I told my grandson that he had put his shoes on the wrong feet and he replied, "But granddad, they're the only feet I have".

I see in Egypt, they now have drive thru pyramids. The sign outside says 'Toot and come in'.

A pirate asked a tatooist how much would it cost to have his ears pierced. The tattooist replied "A buck an ear".

A black country person was knocked unconscious and came round in hospital. He asked the nurse if he had come here to die. She replied, "No, you came in yesterday".

A group of people from the black country were travelling in Monmouthshire when the driver said "Look at that". One of the passengers said "Tintern Abbey" of which the driver said "Tis an Abbey".

A black country guy took his cat to the vets. The vet asks "Is it a tom?" Of which the guy responds "No, it's here with me".

Took my old Cluedo set to the charity shop today. When I handed it over, I told them it was always Colonel Mustard that did it. They said "Why did you give the game away?"

Doing some decorating today, I knocked a tin of paint over me. I was overcome with emulsion.

A pie was standing on the corner of a street. He was meetin' potato.

Had a game of darts last night. My mate said "Nearest the bull wins". He went "Baah", I went "Moo". I won.

Trafalgar Day fact – Nelson was 5' 6" in real life. His statue in Trafalgar Square is 17' 4". That a Horatio of around 3 to 1.

I was having a tattoo of an Indian on my back when I reminded the tattooist "Don't forget the tomahawk". He replied "Give me chance, I haven't finished his turban yet".

Went to the zoo yesterday and I saw a bloke chatting to a cheetah. I thought, "Hello, he's trying to pull a fast one".

Police have arrested a woman for stealing a sign reading "& Emergency". She claimed she found it by Accident.

I don't know why I just bought some new coconut shampoo. I haven't even got any coconuts.

I saw a psychologist fall over the other day. It was a Freudian slip.

I've just been accused of being a plagiarist. Their words, not mine.

I left my last girlfriend because she wouldn't stop counting. I wonder what she's up to now.

Neil Armstrong's initials are not applicable to me.

Before the 'Iron Age' I wonder if everything was just creased.

My wife & daughter are leaving me because of my obsession with horse racing. And they're off.

As a child, I was forced to walk the plank. We couldn't afford a dog.

To be honest all this hype about the weather today is a bit disappointing. It's nothing compared to 'The great storm of me leaving the toothpaste lid off last Tuesday'.

Accident on the M4 today was between a lorry containing a load of tortoises crashing in to a van carrying a load of terrapins. Police said it was a turtle disaster.

On my way home last night, I got stuck behind a slow moving tractor. The driver was leaning out of his cab shouting "The world is going to end, the world is going to end". Then I realised, it was Farmer Geddon.

I had my meters read earlier, there were no real surprises. They were all 100cm.

I just saw a notice board with the word 'bad' advertised on it. I thought "That's not a good sign".

"Time is a construct of man, a means of adding value and structure to a chaotic universe, it serves no real purpose, it's endless and infinite, unfathomable and subjective". "I'm not bothered, you're still late" replied my boss.

Just been watching the news and apparently police are holding three men over a fire in West London. Bit harsh, I wonder what they've done.

I tried to steal Halloween pillows from the supermarket yesterday. It had grim reaper cushions.

Just had a phone call from the manager of the double glazing firm that installed our windows a year ago saying that he hadn't received payment yet. I replied that the sales rep at the time said "In a years time they would pay for themselves". The phone went quiet.

Hammie the World's oldest Hamster has died at the age of 23. Apparently he fell asleep at the wheel.

Clones are people two.

I was asked today why I was only wearing one glove on my hand. I explained that I listened to the weather forecast that morning, and they said that it was going to be warm today, but on the other hand it could be cold.

When I was a kid, I wanted to be a vet. Apparently, I was too young.

I was stood in the library yesterday and a bloke came in and attacked me with a swede and took the novel I was holding. I thought "That's a turnip for the books".

Some years ago I caught the train from Malmo to Stockholm and during the journey I went to the buffet for a drink. I was very surprised to see several youths dressed in "Teddy Boy" suits. I got chatting to one of them and he explained that rock and roll was very popular in Sweden. They were all quite pleasant apart from one named Ulf who was extremely rude. At one point Ulf grabbed a beer from the bar and took a mouthful and threw it all over the barman. I said to Olaf, the chap I had spoken to earlier, that this was not a very nice way to behave. He replied, "Yes, it is terrible, but it is well known throughout the world that.......rude Ulf the Ted loathes train beer...."

'When one door closes another one opens'. Bloody useless kitchen fitters.

They say we are going to have heavy rain today. What I would like to know is, who weighs it?

There's a zebra crossing at the end of our cul-de-sac. Strange place to put a zoo.

My dad turned 80 yesterday. I took him clubbing with me as he'd never been to one. While we were there we both took some speed. Never again, though. I can't stand discos with non-stop oldies.

I rang my mate Stan and his wife answered."I wanted to wish you and Stan a good holiday", I said. "You fly from Gatwick tomorrow, don't you?" She said, "Stansted". "Blimey", I thought, "He seemed absolutely fine in the pub last night". RIP Stan.

I was walking through a field in Afghanistan with my mate when I spotted a silver disc on the ground. As I bent down to pick it up, my mate stopped and shouted "Stop! That's a mine!" I said "Bullshit. Finders keepers! Anyway why you suddenly talking like an Italian?"

I went on a date with a blonde woman last night. "Do you have any kids?" she asked.
"Yes" I replied. "I have one child that's just under two". She said, "I might be blonde, but I know how many one is".

A bloke just knocked on my door. He was about 3ft 3ins tall. "Who are you?" I asked. He replied, "I'm the metre man".

I'm thinking of starting a new band called 1023m because I don't think we'll get a gig.

According to serving suggestions, I'm a family of four.

I asked my boss if I could work from home today, but he said that I couldn't. I hate being a pilot.

When my dog had to have his foot amputated, I tried to replace it with one from a toy dog. To be honest, it was a paw substitute.

Whilst walking down the high street earlier, a canvasser approached me and said, "I'm sorry to stop you sir", of which I replied, "Don't worry, you haven't", and carried on walking.

I went to the Chinese last night and ordered numbers 1, 7, 11, 19 and 27. I took them back though as they tasted odd.

Two cannibals eating a clown, one said to the other, "Does this taste funny to you?"

Budgies at the aviary, fed up of not getting an evening meal like the bigger birds do, are to go on strike. They're demanding parrot tea.

My gran struggles to get up and down the stairs these days so I had a stairlift installed for her. She doesn't like it very much, in fact, it drives her up the wall.

It's come to light that the spacecraft 'India' launched to Mars indeed had a secret astronaut on board. Reports are coming in that he is very happy and over the moon.

My next door neighbour was slumped over his lawnmower crying his eyes out. He said he would be fine, he was just going through a rough patch.

I met this dwarf called Peter yesterday, he's a baker and he was telling me all about baking flatbreads. It was quite fascinating. I love to hear the pita patter of tiny Pete.

Chinese takeaway £14
Petrol to pick it up £2
Getting home to realise they have forgotten one of your containers – riceless.

I just got attacked by some luggage. The police told me it was a severe case.

Insomnia sufferers – only three more sleeps to Christmas.

I was going to make a joke about carpentry but can't think of any that wood work.

Last night I had to change a lightbulb. A bit later on I crossed the road and walked in to a bar. My life is just one big joke.

I hate my job maintaining childrens playgrounds but the benefits package and pension scheme is really good. Oh well, swings and roundabouts I suppose.

I used to run a campsite for anorexics, but we had to close. Our members were very thin on the ground.

Reports are coming in of a huge explosion in a baking powder factory. Police are expecting casualties to rise.

I stole the punctuation keys from a judges' pc recently. I'm expecting a long sentence.

My Chinese neighbour just told me that he's bought a crows shop. I asked, "Don't you me a clothes shop?" He replied, "A crows shop". "Ok" I said, "I'll come and have a rook later".

A man has died after his angry wife penetrated him with a vegetable. Hell hath no fury like a womans corn.

Met an interesting guy last night who apparently invented the crossword. Didn't catch his name but it was P something T something R.

I tried to sell a second hand clock but I had to withdraw it from sale because of the amount of people asking me if it was a wind up.

I was hit in the face with a television controller today. It wasn't even remotely funny.

It's shocking how people are resuscitated after a heart attack.

I had some spare cash so I invested in purchasing some tennis balls. There is a high rate of returns.

As the enormous clock at work struck nine this morning, I couldn't help thinking to myself, "I should have used longer screws".

I need someone who can sort out a wheel on my bike. All the metal bits on it have come out. Does the cycling association have a spokesperson?

There was a fire on the second floor of my building today. Even though the firemen poured thousands of gallons of water on the blaze, sadly four people still died. The family on the first floor couldn't swim.

Because my boss at the exotic bird sanctuary hates me, he gives me the job of debugging the parrots. Honestly, I'm sick of the polly ticks here.

As I stood at the British Airways desk last night, swaying from side to side, the guy asks, "Can I help you sir?" "Yes", I slurred, unzipping my superman costume and pulling out my wallet, "One ticket to Bristol please". He replied, "You're unable to fly sir, you're far too drunk". I said, "I know mate, that's why I'm getting a plane".

Tea is for mugs.

My neighbour rang the bell this morning, "You couldn't give me a lift to work could you, the front wheel fell off?" he said. It's a nightmare living next to a clown.

I've always had a fear of trolls, but I'm not in a hurry to cure my phobia. I'll cross that bridge when I come to it.

I landed a contract as the Queens hairdresser. I pulled up outside Buckingham Palace and a policeman said, "Have you got a permit?" "No" I said, "I've just got to give her a trim".

Just got back from Tesco where a bloke started throwing cheddar cheese at me. I said, "That's not very mature is it?"

Just got back from Tesco where a bloke started throwing cheese, eggs, butter and milk at me. How dairy.

Went to a funeral today and during the graveside service noticed some pallbearers pass by. A few minutes later, they came back and passed us again. After the service, they were still carrying their coffin around. I thought to myself "They've lost the plot".

Tom, Dick and Harry are building a skyscraper when Tom falls off and is killed instantly. Harry is sent to break the news to his wife. Two hours later, Harry comes back carrying a six pack. "Where did you get the beer?" asks Dick. "Toms wife gave it to me", replies Harry. "That's unbelievable", says Dick, "You told the lady her husband is dead and she gives you beer?" "Not exactly", replied Harry. When she answered the door, I said to her, "You must be Toms widow". She said, "I'm not a widow". And I said, "Want to bet me a six pack?"

I bought a new shrub trimmer today. It's cutting hedge technology.

My mobile phone has just filmed a 3 hour documentary about life inside my pocket.

With great reflexes comes great response ability.

Spoiler alert: The wing just fell off the back of my car.

My mate offered to give me a lift. No use to me, I live in a bungalow.

The Isle of Dogs is the Isle of Mans' best friend.

I'm neutral about Switzerland, but their flag is a big plus.

Every morning when I get out of bed, I stand with my left foot slightly raised in the air. It helps me start the day off on the right foot.

I've just been on Trip Advisor. There's no information at all about grazed knees or twisted ankles.

Last time I try and buy any drugs in an Indian restaurant. They sold me curry powder instead. I was in a korma for a week.

I'm having trouble finding out what 51, 6 and 500 are in roman numerals. I'm LIVID.

The Wife

My wife asked me for a pet spider for her birthday, so I went to our local pet shop and they were £70. "Blow this", I thought, "I can get one cheaper off the web".

Just sat down in the restaurant and I've ordered the hippo soup. Not sure what I'm going to have yet.

My wife dropped her epilepsy medicine in the washing machine. Her clothes don't fit anymore.

I looked out of my window and saw a guy in a black robe who was trying to clear the frost off his car with a scythe. So I thought I'd go and help. "Stop", said my wife, grabbing my arm. "You're de-icing with death".

I woke the wife up this morning by smacking her round the head with a thousand piece jigsaw. "What did you do that for?" She said, looking puzzled.

Got my wife some lovely perfume for Xmas. It's called tester, hope she likes it.

The wife said to me, "You haven't listened to a word I've said have you?" I thought, "That's a strange way of starting a conversation".

I cremated my wifes pet and made a plaque out of it to celebrate our anniversary. It was a cat ash trophy.

My wife found out that I'd been moving her bookmark forward a few pages every night. She really lost the plot.

I phoned my wife earlier. "I'm just setting off from work, do you want me to pick up fish and chips on my way home?" It was met with a stony silence. I think she still regrets letting me name the twins.

Tonight my wife came home from work crying and asked me to console her. So I hit her over the head with my Xbox !

After saying she was leaving me for constantly being sarcastic, my wife said "Do you know the difference between you and I?" "Yes" I said. "12 letters".

My wife has been having a go at me for leaving a rusty old car on our driveway for over a year. Now she has said, "Until you get rid of it there is no more sex". Does anyone want to buy a 1994 Ford Fiesta, no MOT, no Tax, 194,500 miles, £23,000 O.N.O.

My wife came up to me with tears streaming down her face. She looked at me and muttered, "You aren't the man I married." I said, "Bloody hell, your Alzheimers is getting out of hand".

My wife got me going when she told me all she was buying me for Christmas was a clockwork toy car. Turned out to be a wind-up.

Looking at my wife lying in bed this morning reminded me it won't be long until Christmas day. She looked like a pig in a blanket.

Last night my wife sent me a text, saying she was in casualty. When I got home I watched all 50 minutes of it, never saw her once. She still hasn't come home yet. I'm starving.

Every time you talk to your wife, you should remember that 'This conversation will be recorded for quality and training purposes'.

My wife said she was leaving me due to my obsession with the 60's group The Monkees.
I thought she was joking, and then I saw her face.

My wife has just gone to her Xmas fancy dress party dressed up as a can of pet food.
She was done up like a dog's dinner.

I woke up this morning at 8 and could smell something was wrong. I got downstairs and found the wife face down on the kitchen floor, not breathing. I panicked. I didn't know what to do. Then I remembered, Wetherspoons serve breakfast until 11.30.

So the wife said to me last night "There's no spark between us any more", so I tasered her, I'll ask her again when she comes round.

The police came to my front door last night holding a picture of my wife. They said "Is this your wife sir?" Shocked, I answered "Yes." They said "I'm afraid it looks like she's been hit by a bus." I said "I know, but she's good with the kids".

I went to see the Red Arrows yesterday. There were gasps of "Ooh" and "Aah" as the crowds watched on in amazement. Near miss after near miss had some people covering their eyes and shaking their heads in disbelief. It was a good half hour's worth of entertainment, but in the end, my wife finally managed to park the car and we made our way to the air show.

The wife has just come home from hospital after having a breast reduction operation, and I must say, she does look a lot better with just the two.

My missus crashed her car into some guy last night. She told the police the guy had been on his mobile and drinking a beer from a can at the time. The police said he was entitled to do what he wanted to do in his own conservatory.

My wife told me to take a spider out instead of killing it. We went and had drinks. Cool guy, wants to be a web designer.

"Do you remember that row we had twenty years ago when we sat down and wrote down each others faults?" I said to my wife. "Oh God yes, I still have mine somewhere", she said with a laugh. "I've just finished mine", I replied.

My missus was reading a magazine earlier when she shoved it in my face and showed me a picture of an expensive coat. "I'd really like that" she said, so I cut it out and gave it to her.

The wife said she was feeling light-headed due to a low iron level. To help her, I raised the ironing board to a more suitable height.

The wife came home with four cases of beer, three boxes of wine, two bottles of whisky and two loaves of bread. "Are we expecting guests?" I asked. "No," she replied."Then why did you buy so much bread?"

I thought I saw the wife out in the back yard this morning, jabbering away to herself. But it was just the wheelie bin lid blowing up and down in the wind.

Having my ears syringed is one of the most painful things I've ever had done. I can hear my wife perfectly now.

The wife complains I never buy her flowers. I never knew she sold them.

I've started calling my Mrs 'Aston Villa' because she kicks off every ten minutes.

Me and the wife have just watched 3 dvds back to back. Fortunately, I was the one facing the tv.

I asked the wife to describe me in 5 words. She said I'm mature, I'm moral, I'm pure, I'm polite, I'm perfect. She then added I also had a fundamental lack of understanding about apostrophes and spaces.

I held the door open for a gorgeous blonde last night. My wife said "You never do that for me". I replied, "What about that time you threatened to leave?"

Just got the wife a matching bag and belt set for her birthday. Let's hope the hoover works better now.

My pregnant wife and me were travelling through Kurdistan when she gave birth to our baby son. "You do realise", my wife said, "That because he was born here, he would be a Kurd ?" I replied, "It's not a Kurd to me yet".

I left my wife because she wouldn't stop counting. I often wonder what she's up to now.

My wife has just got a job working in Boots. She's a prostitute.

I was all covered in bubble wrap and on my way out the door when my wife said," Where do you think you're going?" I said, "Just popping off to the pub".

I was devastated when I got home from the shops today to find that my wife had left me. I had just bought a seesaw.

My wife is threatening to leave because of my obsession to become a tailor. I said "Fine, suit yourself".

Just took my missus out. What a great shot it was.

My wife is a magician. She can turn anything in to an argument.

Booked a table for Valentines day. Hope it's better than last year, she only managed to pocket 2 balls.

Winds of 108mph, structural damage, flying debris, massive depression, icy blasts, communication difficulties, untold misery and suffering. Yes, I forgot the valentines card again.

Every night when I'm asleep, my wife takes all the money out of my trousers. I think she's going through the change.

The wife is getting angry because I won't stop my flamingo impressions. So, I've had to put my foot down.

My wife left me because I'm so insecure. No, wait, she's back. She'd just gone to make a cup of tea.

My wife threatened to leave me because of my obsession with horse racing. And she's off.

My wife has threatened to leave me just because I've installed cctv cameras all around the house. I can she where's she coming from.

I love playing mind games with my wife. Today I bought her some flowers and I haven't even done anything wrong.

My wife says that I'm obsessed with Facebook. Well how do you like that?

My wife says that I'm useless at fitting electrical appliances. Well she's in for a shock.

My wife is leaving me because of my obsession with dried fruit. Fine, whilst she's rasin our kids, I'll find a date.

I said to my wife, "What would you do if I won the Lotto?" She says, "I'd take half, then leave you". "Excellent", I replied, "I won £12, here's £6, now sod off".

My missus said, "I think I've got a stone in my shoe". I thought, more like 20 stone you lardarse.

My wife had a terrible fear of spiders, so I booked her in with a hypnotist hoping he could cure her. She only went for 5 sessions as it seemed to do the trick. Trouble is now though, she's scared of tripods.

My wife just got a tattoo of a drinking flask on her arm. Apparently the plumber told her she needed to get a new Thermos-tat before he could fix the boiler.

Me and the wife have invented a collision avoidance system for our car. I'm calling it the iDrive.

"I've had enough of your stupid pipe dreams", shouted my wife as she stormed out the room. I sat in my chair emotionless, pretending to smoke my pipe.

My wife said to me last night, "Can you explain why I've just found a pair of womens knickers in your coat pocket?" I said, "Yes I can .... It's because you're nosey".

My wife was reversing on to the driveway today, looking at all the neighbours gardens and moaning about the state of them. She's such a nosey parker.

My wife turned off the TV whilst I was watching it today. After a few moments of staring at the blank screen, I thought to myself, "That's not on".

I think the wife is doing salad for tea tonight. Either that or the smoke alarm is broke.

Turn a regular sofa in to a bed sofa, just by forgetting your wifes birthday.

I really thought my wife was going to get me something unique for tonight's fancy dress. Unfortunately, all she got me was a black hooded robe and a scythe. Things are looking Grim.

Just found a bag in my wifes car that has ' Sorry , it was my fault and it won't happen again' written across it. I think it's her make-up bag.

"I see you've woken up on the wrong side of the bed", said my wife this morning.
"I know", I replied, "Get the mattress off me please".

My wife asked me why I was painting the number 17 on our dustbin when in fact our number is 49. I replied, "So that when the bin men come, there's a better chance it will end up nearer our house when they've emptied it".

My wife says I'm lazy, just because I hired a secretary at work. "Lazy!" I proclaimed, "She's only dealing with my mail". "I know", she replied, "But you're a postman".

I met my wife whilst speed dating. I said "What are you doing here?"

"Why do we always end up playing 'Monopoly'?" asked my wife. I had to admit that I didn't have a cluedo.

The wife told me an up-to-date Marathon joke earlier that was quite funny. Had me Snickering.

My wife complained of me being OCD yesterday. I soon put her in her place.

Almost lost two teeth at teatime this evening. The wife had done a Lego lamb.

I walked in to the bosses office and handed him a pear. "What's this for?" he asked. "A pay rise" I replied, "My wife told me to grow it first and then ask you".

My wife was counting all the 1p's and 2p's out on the kitchen table when she suddenly got very angry and started shouting and crying for no reason. I thought to myself "She's going through the change".

My wife and I were talking about obscure animals. She said "I've always wanted to get a manatee". I said "That's very nice of you, milk and two sugars please".

My wife was complaining that it was too dark in the kitchen so I told her to turn the light on.
I'm full of bright ideas.

I asked my wife to buy me some cod today but she came back with some sort of fish that cost half the price. Bloody cheapskate.

"Your driving is awful" I said to my wife this morning. "It would help if you told me where I should be going" she yelled. "Do I go left at the roundabout, or do I go right?" "Do a left" I replied calmly, "Then do a right between the swings and the slide".

I've finally managed to stop the wife worrying about me leaving her for someone else. I've left her for someone else.

I came home from work today to find my wife and her fat friends sitting on the settee and chairs eating pizza, chips and garlic bread. I muttered under my breath "Fat cows". My wife said, "I beg your pardon?" I replied, "You herd".

My wife just text me, "What's this I hear about you being in bed with Mrs A. Who is she?" I text back, "It's MRSA you tart".

My wife has just started going through the change. It's going to be really weird calling her Dave.

My wife left me to work for the tourist board on a tropical island. She sells Seychelles by the sea shore.

My wife was lecturing me because I kept deducting her score in scrabble for no reason. "Point taken" I replied.

I always carry a picture of my wife and kids in my wallet. It reminds me of why there's never any money in it.

My wife and I have just learned how to speak both Terrapin and Turtle from our new pet.
He taught us.

My wife got a ladder in her tights. She truly is the most talented shoplifter ever.

I said to my wife "I'm worried that those plants in the corner of the greenhouse are artificial". "They're not" she replied. "Well that's a real leaf then".

My wife said she's leaving me because I'm too clingy. "Ok", I said, "I'll come with you".

"You talk in your sleep" said my wife. "Really?" I replied, "That's probably because it's the only time I can actually get a word in".

My wife laughed her head off when I said that I was going to build a motorcycle made out of spaghetti. You should have seen here face when I rode pasta.

My wife just left me because I watch too many 'Who wants to be a millionaire'. I was so distraught I had to phone a friend.

My mate said he downloaded an app that tracks his drinking and eating habits. I do it the old fashioned way...A nagging wife.

Just been to Tescos with the wife and right out of the blue she called me a right lazy so and so. I nearly fell out of the trolley.

I've just learned that if you upset your wife, she nags you, but if you upset her further, you get the silent treatment. Does anyone else think it's worth that little extra effort?

I made my wifes' dream come true and we were wed in a castle. But you wouldn't have thought it by the look on her face when we were bouncing around.

My wife often complains that I don't listen to her, and that I am not attentive to her knees.

I gave my wife £50 and told her to go out on Thursday and leave me in peace while I watched World Cup football. "I won't need that much" she laughed. "You will," I said. "It's got to last you five weeks".

I was watching the football last night when my wife said, "It's about time you did some jobs around the house". She's right, of course, but I think she's losing it. They say talking to yourself is the first sign of madness.

I went in to the kitchen this morning and said to my wife "Is that coffee I smell?" She replied, "It is, and you do".

I came downstairs this morning to find the wife cooking our breakfast in her slippers. I really must get her a frying pan.

My wife just had a go at me saying that I never listen to her. Or something like that.

My wife demanded that I called an electrician to fix the plug but I re-fused.

My wife just spent 4hrs painting tiny timepieces on to each of her finger nails. I told her she had too much time on her hands.

After criticising yet another outfit, my wife said she was going to leave me due to my poor dress sense. "Please baby" I pleaded. "I can change".

According to Tetley, the best way to make a cup of tea is to agitate the bag. So every morning I slap the wife on the arse and say "Two sugars fatty".

My wife called me a juvenile loser just because I turned our house into a 'Fun House'.
I'm not sure why, maybe she just got out of bed on the wrong slide.

My wife and I tried roast badger with all the trimmings at our local restaurant last night. We had the sett meal for two.

The wife was really restless in bed tonight. I bet there's a cake in the fridge.

Our young son has been crying a lot at night so my wife told me to go out and get a baby monitor for him. He seems even more freaked out now that a lizard is crawling all over him.

"You will never know what it is like to be a woman", yelled my wife."That's very unfair" I replied, "Sometimes my mind goes blank as well you know".

Realising that my wife would be exhausted when she got in from work, I ran the hot water and made sure there were plenty of bubbles. Now she can do the dishes as soon as she gets home.

My wife is always moaning she wanted a real animal skin coat, so for her birthday I've got her a donkey jacket.

My wife is getting ready to go out. She said "Can you see my boobs, should I wear a bra?" I said "Yes, either that or a longer dress".

My wife has left me because of my obsession with pasta. I'm feeling cannelloni right now.

My wife, being unhappy with my mood swings, bought me one of these mood rings so she could monitor my mood. We discovered that, when I am in a good mood, it turns green and, when I am in a bad mood, it leaves a big red mark on her forehead.

My wife, who didn't really want to go to the play I'd bought tickets for, took great delight in telling me it had been cancelled. "Alright" I said "No one likes a show off".

My wife just got out of the shower and asked me what I liked best, her pretty face or her sexy body. I looked her up & down & replied "Your sense of humour". On another note, the new Southmead Hospital is coming along nice, I can just about see it through these swollen eyes.

I took my wife for a drive. Don't know why I did that, she looks nothing like tarmac.

My wife has just found out that I replaced our bed with a trampoline. She hit the roof.

When my wife discovered that my 'little man' was shaped like a space rocket, she was over the moon.

I got home to find my bags had been packed by my missus. On my way out of the front door, she screamed "I wish you a slow and painful death". I replied, "So, you want me to stay then now do you?"

I like to have a smoke after a good meal. Thanks to my wife I don't smoke.

After having surgery a few years ago, the wife is still struggling to breathe through her nose at night. It's really challenging because it requires her to keep her mouth shut.

I've been playing a few pranks on the missus recently. Last night I replaced her sleeping tablets with laxatives just before we got into bed. Unfortunately it back fired on me.

My wife told me she wanted to become one of those, 'Human Barbies'. So I chucked some petrol on her, set her on fire and tried to cook some sausages & burgers on her.

My wife claimed to be fantastic at multi-tasking, well she's only just gone and proved herself right too. She reversed the car and smashed it into a wall all at the same time.

My wife said that the neighbours were planting pickled onions. She was correct, they were planting onions in between lots of beer slug traps.

I used to have a woodpecker called Woody, until he attacked my wife. I still can't believe Woody would peck her.

When I went away on business, the wife said "Don't forget to write". Very unlikely, it's a basic skill.

My wife has just warned me if I don't drop my Eric Morecambe obsession, she'll be on her wahay.

My wife asked me to give her some peace and quiet whilst she was cooking tonights evening meal, so I took the batteries out of the smoke alarm.

I bought a boat without my wife's permission today. I've already named it. The "For Sale" is absolutely beautiful.

Got in from work last night and said "What's that smell?" Wifey said "I can't smell anything". I replied "Exactly, get that oven on".

I told my wife that she'd drawn her eyebrows on too high. She looked surprised.

My wife found out I was cheating when she found the letters I was hiding. She's never going to play scrabble with me again.

I broke up with my wife of twenty five years when I got a job as an astronaut. "I just need space", I said.

My wife complained that the magic had gone out of our relationship. So I cut her in half.

My wife can be so annoying at times. "When are you going to paint the kitchen? When are you going to paint the kitchen? When are you going to paint the kitchen?" Three times I've asked her and she still hasn't done it.

Wondering where to take my wife, I chose a restaurant that specialised in cannabis fed venison. She thought it was a really good high deer.

This morning I threw a massive sirloin at my wifes' head. It went nowhere near her but she got really angry. It was a big missed steak.

My wife was late home from work tonight saying that she was ambushed by a group of men who proceeded to repair her shoes. Sounds like a load of cobblers to me.

I came home today to find my wife on e-bay again. My kids have a weird sense of humour.

My wife left me because I wouldn't let her get a word in edgeways. She can argue all she wants, but I'm sure there's a rule against that in Scrabble.

I said to my wife, "By the end of today, we'll finally be in the black". "Why, have we got enough money to pay off the overdraft?" she asked. "No" I said, "We don't have enough money to pay the electric bill".

My wife took my name when we got married. Now no one knows what to call me.

To this day, I have always thought back to the moment my Spanish wife left without saying goodbye. Not a deigo's bye.

I was chilling with the wife last night. We seriously need to get the central heating sorted.

Well I've never been more organised for Christmas. I told my wife I was getting her a gold bracelet for Christmas and she said "Nothing would please her more". Nothing it is then, sorted.

The wife and I moved in to a tree-house. We soon fell out.

My wife has just turned the television off. I thought to myself, "That's not on".

My wife said if I took one more picture of her she'd leave me. That's when I snapped.

I thought my wife was happy to fully repair my jeans. Or at least sew it seems.

My wife came home and noticed her collection of Elvis records were missing.
"Our pet lizard escaped and ate them" I told her.
"Don't lie" she shouted "Where are they?"
"In the gecko" I replied.

Tonight a friend asked if he could crash on my couch. I had to explain to him I was married now and that's where I sleep.

"All you ever talk about is golf" my wife shouted. "Golf, golf and more bloody golf" "Calm down love" I said, "Don't let this driver wedge between us".

I'm thinking of asking my ex wife to re-marry me. But I'm worried she might be thinking I'm only after her for my money.

Over breakfast this morning, my wife told me she was leaving me because of my obsession with twitter. I was so shocked, I almost choked on my #brown.

I know I can count on my wife. She always wears beads.

Just been watching The Lion, The Witch and The Wardrobe. My wife and her mother have come back from Ikea with a flatpack.

The wife and I had words last night, but I didn't get to use mine.

I'll never understand my wife. She works at the railway station as an announcer for arrivals and departures.

I'm sick of my wife taking the mickey out of me in front of her mates, saying I look like Quasimodo. Don't worry, I'll get my own back.

My wife fell down a ladder and started crying her eyes out. "Lighten up" I said, "It's only a board game".

I slept in my wifes' knickers last night. They make a wonderful hammock.

The wife said "You never listen to me properly and you never give me compliments"
"Rubbish" I replied, "I passed you the salt and pepper last night".

A prayer:-
Dear Lord,
You gave me childhood, and you took it away,
You gave me youth, and you also took that away,
You gave me a wife,
It's been years now,
So, just reminding you.

I always read my wifes horoscope to see what kind of day I'm going to have.

My wife asked "Have you seen my flip flops?" I replied "Of course I have, now put your bra back on".

Alcohol

The barmaid said, "If you're going in the beer garden you'll have to use plastic glasses".
"Forget that, I just paid £200 for these from Specsavers", I replied.

I came home from the pub four hours late last night. "Where the hell have you been?" screamed my wife. I said, "I've been playing poker with some blokes". "Playing poker with some blokes?" she repeated. "Well, you can pack your bags and go" "So can you", I said. "This isn't our house anymore".

I went to a fancy dress party as a Spider last night. Christ knows what time I crawled in at.

I've worked for thirty years inspecting the fire exits of country pubs all across the country.
I know all the inns and outs of my job.

It's true when they say that certain types of music can take you to another place. I was in the pub last night and a One Direction song was playing on the jukebox, so I went to another pub.

Bill & Ben went in the pub. Bill says "flob a dob a lob", Ben says, "I'll get these, you're drunk".

I think I promised to have 3 beers and be in by 10. I always get those 2 mixed up.

My boss told me that there are no such things as problems, only opportunities. I said "Great, in that case, I have a serious drinking opportunity".

I was at a party last night and got in the queue for the alcoholic fruit drink. Everybody was waiting their turn without any pushing or rudeness. I thought, "Finally, a decent punchline".

Was in the pub last night and telling my mates the joke about, what would you do if an epileptic was having a fit in the bath....... throw your washing in .... The bloke on the next table said, "My brother who's epileptic had a fit in the bath and died"...... Well if the ground could swallow me up. I apologised and asked him if he drowned? He said "No, he choked on a sock".

We have a 99 year old man in our pub darts team so as a surprise we are going to fulfil his wish of spending his centenary birthday in the Caribbean. He's going to be 100 in Haiti.

Nurse:noun.(n3-rs) The first person you see after saying "Here, hold my beer and watch this".

I just drank some wkd with ice in it. It was wicked.

I bought an alcoholic ginger beer. He wasn't pleased.

I went to a new pub last night which featured a network of paths and hedges designed as a puzzle through which one had to find a way to the bar. It was a Maze Inn.

Does anyone know which page in the bible explains how to turn water in to wine? It's for a party this weekend.

A bloke walks in the pub and sees three men and a dog playing poker. I said to the landlord, "That's a clever dog". The landlord replied, "Not really, every time he gets a good hand his tail starts wagging".

On my way home from the off licence earlier, I dropped my bag in a puddle. It really dampened my spirits.

I was in the pub last night talking to a couple of bouncers when the barmaid rudely interrupted and said "Will you talk to my face and not my boobs?"

I probably shouldn't have driven home from the pub last night, especially as I walked there in the first place.

When I was in the pub tonight I overheard a couple of blokes saying that they wouldn't feel safe on an aircraft if they knew the pilot was a woman. What a pair of sexist gits. I mean, it's not as if she'd have to reverse the bloody thing.

I was so drunk coming back from the pub last night that I spent nearly half an hour trying to get my front door key in the lock. That's when I stood back, took a deep breath & thought to myself, "I don't even live in this post box".

I was so drunk last night that I didn't know if I had found some car keys or lost a car.

My local landlord is a 'glass half full' kind of guy...or a useless barman as he's better known.

My daughter's hamster escaped from its cage last night so I spent 4 hours looking for it.
No luck though, he definitely wasn't in the pub.

"I wouldn't drink that Stowford Cider if I were you mate" I said to some bloke stood at the bar last night, "It'll make your teeth fall out." "Really?" he asked. I said, "Yes mate, that's my pint".

A man walked into a bar with a newt on his shoulder. "What do you call it?" asked the barman. "Tiny" the man replied. "Why Tiny?" the barman asked. "Because he's my newt".

Two cigarettes sitting in a pub having a drink when another cigarette walks in. "Don't mess about with him" said one cigarette to the other, "He's menthol".

Every time I drink Magners or Bulmers I start swearing. Must be some kind of Cider Fecks.

I was having a pint in the Bricklayers Arms last night when I thought to myself "I'd better let him get on and finish this wall off".

Had a really heavy night drinking last night, only to be woken at 06:30 this morning with the neighbour mowing his lawn. I felt like punching his lights out, but then thought "Nah, let him mow round me".

I went into the pub & asked if they did cash back.
"Yes we do" replied the barmaid.
"Good, can I have the £50 I spent last night, the wifes' going mental?" I answered.

A bartender who came last in a cocktail competition has been involved in a serious accident.
He's ok, just been badly shaken.

I've just bought some shares in Thatchers, now I've been done for in-cider trading.

A snake went in to a bar and asked the barman for a pint. "I'm sorry" said the barman, "I can't serve you, you can't hold your drink".

I'm not normally by nature an inquisitive person, but I would still be interested to know why last Saturday morning I woke up in a wheelie bin, naked and smeared with peanut butter.

An elderly man was stopped by the police around 2 a.m. and was asked where he was going at that time of night. The man replied, "I'm on my way to a lecture about alcohol abuse and the effects it has on the human body, as well as smoking and staying out late". The officer then asked, "Really? Who's giving that lecture at this time of night?" The man replied, "That would be my wife".

I was so drunk last night that I 'crashed out' on the settee. My wife come down the stairs stark naked and decided she was going to take advantage of me. She nicked my wallet.

Walking home from the pub last night and someone shot me with a starting pistol. Police are saying it's a race related incident.

My wife spends every night going in to town and going to pub after pub……………..and she always ends up finding me.

A brain walks in to the pub and asks for a pint. The landlord said "I'm not serving you, you're already out of your head".

A mate of mine text me the other day saying he'd had such a heavy nights drinking last Friday, and it was only when he woke up Saturday morning, next to a fat, old, spotty woman that he'd realised he'd made it home safely.

Coffee makes people really aggressive. Last night I had 10 pints in the pub whilst my wife had two coffees at home. You should've seen how pissed off she was.

A 74 year old woman has visited 972 Wetherspoon pubs throughout the UK. When asked when she was going to stop, she replied, "When I find a good one".

An IRA victim that has been missing since 1978 has been found dead in an Irish bog. Judging by the infrequency of cleaning, I'm guessing it's a Wetherspoons.

I was rolling a cigarette on the way home from the pub last night when I thought, "It's got to be quicker to pick it up and carry it".

Got a letter from Vodafone saying my balance is outstanding. They obviously haven't seen me drunk on a Friday night.

I decided to treat myself last night. I was wrecked when I discovered that tin of Ronseal.

When I was young I was a foster child, now I'm older I'm on special brew.

I never drink unless I'm alone, or with somebody.

Came home well drunk last night to find the wife had changed the locks on the doors. Not only that, she had changed the name of the street too.

Did you know it's just as easy to get drunk on water ....as it is on land?

Did you know drunken sex is not allowed in Iceland. They weren't too happy in Farmfoods either.

I got pulled over by the police last night and was ordered to get out of the car. "You're staggering" he said. "You're not sho bad lookin yourshelf" I replied.

I had a bath filled with vodka on the 35th floor of the Hotel I was staying in last night. I was in high spirits.

Dave

My mate Dave says he makes a living conning people into giving him deposits for clothes they will never receive. I reckon he's all mouth and no trousers.

Dave got sacked from the m&m factory because he threw away all the 'W's.

My mate Dave was sacked as he almost fell out of a crane whilst working at the new hospital. He was suspended on medical grounds.

I've just given my mate Dave, who's in prison, a calculator for Christmas. It's what's on the inside that counts.

My mate Dave was rushed into intensive care at the weekend after getting into difficulties swallowing an entire scrabble set. I want to know how he is, but as of yet, there's no word from him.

I hate people who think they're worse off than everyone else. My mate Dave was in an accident and he lost both his legs and the ability to speak, but you don't see him making a song and dance about it.

My mate Date keeps racing pigeons. They always win.

My mate Dave has just drown in a bowl of Muesli. A strong currant pulled him in.

My mate Daves son walked over to our sleeping cat and began gently petting her and telling her that he loves her when out of nowhere, she jumped up, started to hiss and scratched him to bits. Needless to say he ran away crying. On a positive note, at least he's now prepared for marriage.

My mate Dave has got a job cleaning up roads after dark in Bristol. I don't know how he sweeps at night.

My mate Dave set me up on a blind date, but he warned me that she was expecting a baby.
I felt a right idiot sitting in the pub in just a nappy.

In the betting shop and my mate Dave told me to put all my money on a horse called Landfill. Didn't come anywhere, it was a rubbish tip.

My mate Dave was seriously injured trying to leap over a wall while dressed as a clown.
He got no sympathy from me though. It was his own stupid vault.

My mate David is a victim of ID theft. He's now called Dav.

My mate Dave just said to me "What rhymes with orange?" I said "No it doesn't".

My mate Dave died when he saw a wild ox wearing a knitted jumper. It was a cardi yak arrest.

My mate Dave is convinced that he will crash his bike if the tyre pressures aren't always exactly correct. I reckon it's just cycle logical.

My mate Dave asked me not to mention anything about his new girlfriends' lazy eye, so I spent all night complementing her normal eye.

A bloke came up to me and said "Have you got a light mate?" I said "Yes, we call him anorexic Dave".

My mate Dave crashed his car in to a lemon tree a couple of months ago. He's still bitter and twisted.

My mate Dave has drunk many weird and wonderful things. I asked him if he has ever drank cologne. He replied, "No, always with mates".

A man received the following text from his neighbour :-

'I am so sorry Dave, I have been riddled with guilt so much that I have to confess. I have been tapping your wife day and night when you are not around. In fact, more than you. I'm not getting any at home, but that is no excuse. I can no longer live with the guilt and so I hope you will accept my sincere apologies. I promise it won't happen again'.

Dave, anguished and betrayed, went to his bedroom, grabbed his gun and without a word, shot his wife and killed her. A few moments later, a second text came in :-

'Damn autocorrect, "wifi", I meant "wifi", not "wife".

My mate Dave wanted to start smoking but I didn't want to lead him ashtray.

My mate Dave was a ground breaker in his chosen field. Unfortunately for him, that was because the parachute didn't open.

My mate Dave and his work colleagues were all due to run in Sunday's Marathon in aid of injured bus drivers, but they all pulled out without indicating.

I'm not saying my mate Dave is boring, but he could talk a glass eye to sleep.

My mate Dave asked me if I wanted to go into business with him making blunt knives.
I just couldn't see the point.

My mate Dave reckons he's addicted to brake fluid but he can stop at any time.

Last night my mates, Dave, Dan and Steve won the pogo stick championships again.
That's three on the bounce.

My mate Dave hates it when I put his chocolate bars in other chocolate bar wrappers. It gets his snickers in a twix.

My mate Dave keeps taking his clothes off at sporting events and running on the field. I am going to start putting windolene in his food. That should stop him streaking.

My mate Dave was moaning about how he spends so much money on bus fares each month that he can't afford an MP3 player that he's desperate to buy. I said "walk, man."

I went cotton picking with Dave today. I chose Fearne, he chose Dot.

My mate Dave is off to India tomorrow and he reckons that he's going to go on an elephant.
Yeah right, it would take years to get there.

My mate Dave was arrested for drunk driving on a motorized shopping cart at Asda.
Apparently he led the police on a chase that reached 90 aisles per hour.

I always had a suspicion that my mate Dave was racist, but tonight, after a few pints, he finally came out with it and said "I could murder an Indian".

Just got back from my mate Daves funeral. He died after being hit on the head with a tennis ball. It was a lovely service.

Me and my mate Dave were driving round last night looking for a small parcel of earth that was sent to him. Personally, I think he's lost the plot.

Genie "What is your wish?" Dave "I wish I was rich"
Genie "What is your second wish?"
Rich "I want lots of money".

My mate Dave phoned me and asked me what I was doing. I said "Probably failing my driving test".

I've been sitting here watching my mate Daves Woodstock video for the past three hours. How boring was this? Then I realised, he's a night security watchman in a timber yard.

My mate Dave said "Lynx is the best selling deodorant on the market". "Sure is", I replied. "Oh, sorry, my mistake", was his response.

Just got off the phone to my mate Dave. He said he spent the best part of yesterday unblocking a toilet. What was the rest of the day like if that was the best bit?

My mate Daves' wife has just left him. Took his Sky dish and all his Bob Marley records. No woman, no Sky.

I'd like to congratulate my idiot of a mate Dave on becoming the local Mayor. Good job he only attends appointments during the day, else he'd be a night-mayor.

My mate Dave has got a new job crushing coke cans, he says it's soda pressing.

We were only a few minutes into our chess game when Dave said, "After my next move we should go out for a Pilsner Urqell". "Why's that?" I inquired. "Because it's Czech, mate".

I said to my mate Dave, "I can't remember the name of the movie company that has a mountain in its logo" He said, "Is it paramount?" I said, "Not really, it's just really annoying me".

My mate Dave said, "For a laugh, I'll change my name to Pheasant if you change yours to Grouse". I replied, "I'm game if you are".

My mate Dave fell into a vat of strawberry preserve and received £1,000,000 compensation. Jammy sod.

I was walking home from work this evening, when my mate Dave pulled over and gave me a lift. I don't know what I'm going to do with it, I live in a bungalow.

Computers/Technology

I missed most of Apple's roadshow last night at which they unveiled a load of new products on tv. I managed to see the ilights though.

My New Year resolution :- 1600 x 1200.

My son was baptised Times New Roman. I think the vicar used the wrong font.

What do you get if you cross a computer with a hamburger? A big mac.

Just had my dog computer chipped. Now he's full of Terrierbytes.

Did you hear about the word document who has run out of town? He couldn't escape the rumours that he was a PDF file.

The inventor of predictive text has died. His funfair will be hello on monkey.

I changed my iPod's name to Titanic. It's syncing now.

My wife just said that if I keep typing so loudly she is going to slam my face in to the key!sxzcbG;m.

I walked down a street where the houses were numbered 64k, 128k, 256k, 512k and 1mb. It was a trip down memory lane.

I ate a pixelated brownie yesterday. Only took me one byte.

I drove my car into a river and watched it turn into a mobile phone. One minute, a Kia, next minute, Nokia.

Apparently the government has a database containing the details of every single animal attack on humans. Wonder how big it is, probably many terror bites.

I now pronounce you man and wife. You may update your Facebook status.

Someone accused me of not knowing the concept of Skype. I said, "Watch who you're talking to".

Just did a karaoke for a load of mobile phone companies, it was really quiet and not many people wanted to join in, only Sam sung.

I'm Embarrassed to talk about putting a CD into the CD Player. It's Disc Inserting.

I changed my computer password to 'incorrect'. Now whenever I forget what it is, it tells me.

Fix broken keys on your keyboard by using superglue but take care nottttttttttttttttttttttttttttttttt. ....

Dear auto correct, stop correcting my swear words you piece of shut.

My laptop is knackered. It just keeps playing 'Chasing Pavements' over and over again.
Probably because it's a Dell.

Whoever stole my Microsoft Office, I will get revenge. You have my word.

WhatsApp kept crashing on my phone, so I downloaded something called 'The Bugs Bunny' to sort it out. It's a WhatsApp Doc.

Wi-Fi went down today so had to talk to the family. Seem like nice folk.

Whoever stole my external hard drive has got my back up.

Our wi-fi went down today so I had to talk with the wife. I was surprised to hear that she no longer works at Woolworths.

If my iPod doesn't work in the next few minutes, I'm throwing it in the river.
It can either sync or swim.

The internet is an amazing thing. One minute I'm at work looking at random pages passing the time, the next minute I'm at home looking for a new job.

The guy in PC World asked me how much storage space I had on my laptop. "I manage to balance a couple of plates and a mug of tea on it" I said.

Some of my friends secretly downloaded an EXE file on my laptop. It was a setup.

I saw a sheep with a great memory yesterday. 9 gig ram.

I've been trying to buy a train ticket online today for well over an hour now and I'm getting really hacked off. It keeps asking me 'Where do you want to go to?' so I click the icon 'home' and then it makes me start all over again.

Looking at the weather map on my phone, I said "Google, surely it's not going to rain again today is it?" Google replied, "It is and don't keep calling me Shirley". I'd forgotten to take it off Airplane mode.

I've just been told to change my password to 8 characters. Can only think of Snow White and the 7 Dwarfs.

Doesanyoneknowwhatthelongbuttonatthebottomoft hekeyboardisfor?

this is the last 🖕time i buy a keyboard on ebay

Sport

My wife has left me because of my obsession with cricket. It really hit me for six.

The wife said to me "Whenever a world cup game is on let's eat something to do with that team for tea that night". Mexico was on, we had burritos, Japan was on, we had sushi, USA was on, we had burgers, Italy was on, we had pizza. Tonight is England, so we're going out.

We were in the pub last night when my mate Dave came in wearing the most embarrassing shirt ever. "Cost me 50 quid" he said. "I hope you kept your receipt" I said. "Too right" he replied, "I'm going straight back to the Aston Villa club shop tomorrow".

My wife has just left me, saying I love football more than her. I don't know what to do, we'd been married 24 seasons.

My wife said to me, "You're home from work early". I said, "I've got some good news and some bad news. The good news is, I've been promoted". "Great" she exclaimed, "What's the bad news?" Well, I was dancing around, celebrating my promotion, when Dave sacked me on the spot. Apparently, I shouldn't have been playing 'Football Manager' at work.

What time do Aston Villa kick off this week? Every ten minutes.

My local schools caretaker has been fired. A football manager has been appointed until a replacement can be found.

Who will take the second shot in this snooker game? Find out after the break.

Cricket is over-rated.

"Are you watching the game tonight?" my boss asked. "I'm not really interested" I replied. He came back with "I wish you had told me earlier before you had let six goals in before half time".

I've spotted a pattern to when England win the World Cup. It's every 900 years after the Battle of Hastings.

I was just watching live tennis on the internet, this man came from nowhere out of the crowd and ran up to one of the tennis players and smacked him in the face, just as the player was about to throw the ball up into the air. I'd like to tell you more but the servers down at the moment.

Wish me luck in this year's London Marathon. I managed 2 hours, 59 minutes and 33 seconds last year. This year I will try to beat that, but I usually get bored and turn over to watch something else.

My illegal immigrant friend is rubbish at golf. He's got par sport issues.

Told my son to stop hanging around the house and to go out and join a couple of clubs. Only gone and found him soldering my 9 irons.

England are 20/1 to win the World Cup. For those of you who don't understand how odds work, it means if you put £5 on, you lose £5.

The manager of the Red Indian football team is in fear of being sacked. It seems they have had Apache start to their season.

A darts match was taking place in my local last night when the first player threw his first dart in to double top (40). His second dart also went in to double top. As he threw his third dart, a nun came through the door. The dart hit the wire, bounced off the board and hit the nun in the head, killing her instantly. The scorer shouts "One nun dead and eighty".

I was in a Golf Store today and the guy had a huge display of his accessories right in the middle of the shop. I couldn't see the woods for the tees.

I've been told I'm not ambitious enough. If only there was an olympic sport for being a lazy sod. That bronze medal would be mine.

It's a little known fact that Anne Boleyn actually had a brother called Tenpin.

I broke my nose playing baseball in a D.I.Y store car park. I hit homebase.

It's becoming very difficult to meet women at tug-of-war competitions. Everyone's on the pull.

A rare bat has been found in a barn in Essex. It's rumoured to be the one that England used to score runs with.

Two cannibals are at an athletics meeting. "I'm hungry" said the first one. "Me too" agreed the second. "What would you like to eat then?" asked the first. "I think I'll have the starter" replied the second.

I expected a lot more from Greece in the World Cup. They have a lot of big name players.

After Nigeria were eliminated from the World Cup, their goalkeeper personally offered to refund all the expenses of fans that travelled to South Africa. He said he just needs their bank details and pin numbers to complete the transaction.

The police pulled me over today and said that I had to take a test on football stadium capacities. "On what grounds?" I demanded.

It takes a lot of balls to play golf the way I do.

I'm no Tour de France expert but it seems that the best way to win is to wear a yellow t-shirt.

I went to a sports day in Japan today. It was quite enjoyable but I must say the egg and chopstick race was a challenge.

Went by Bodymoor Heath, the aston villa training ground today. The pitch was full of cabbages, then I realised, they were training.

Wanted , football players , anyone who is interested in playing football, must be able to pass / defend , please apply in writing to :-
Aston Villa Football Club,
Birmingham
B6

I managed a personal best in the 100 metres today. I got to 57 metres.

Sky sports will be televising the origami championships next year. It will be on paper view.

Christmas/New Year

"Dad, can I have a phone for Christmas?" "Not unless you finish your yoghurt...now another one .... now get me some string".

HOW TO COOK A TURKEY: First buy a turkey and a bottle of vodka. Pour yourself a glass of vodka and put turkey in the oven. Take another 2 drinks of vodka and set the degree at 375 ovens. Have 3 more vodkas of drink and turn the oven on. Take 4 more vodkas of drink and turk the bastey. Stick a turkey in the therometer and glass youself a pour of vodka. Bake the vodka for 4 hours, take the oven out of the turkey, and floor the turkey up off the pick. Pour yourself another glass of turkey. Now just tet the sable, and turk the carvey!

Just came home to find all my doors have been smashed in, and everything was gone........What sort of sick person does that to someone's Advent calendar?

Frosty the Snowman has been spotted in the vegetable section of the local supermarket. He was seen picking his nose!

When I was part of the Christmas play at school, I was the star of the show. I had no lines and sat at the top of the tree in a stupid yellow costume.

Advent Calendars. Their days are numbered.

So, I've decked the halls as the Christmas song suggested. Not sure Mr & Mrs Hall share my joy though.

M&S new advert states that it wouldn't be Christmas without M&S. They're right, it would be chrita.

Ex football star Michael Owen has released a new fragrance this Xmas. It's set to be called 'My cologne'.

When it comes to small twinkly lights, I'm easily led.

I still remember the day my parents told me that Santa was fake. I was heartbroken. I jumped in my car and went straight to the pub.

Just putting up the Christmas decorations and I've swallowed one. I swear I've got tinselitus.

I broke down on the motorway today. A guy with a big red nose came up asking if he could help. I said "No thanks Santa". He said "I'm not Santa, I'm a chiropodist". I said "In that case, can you give me a tow?"

This Xmas I've bought the perfect gift to show I care. Eye wash.

Do you prefer
Warm wine
Hot cider
I don't care
This is a mull tipple choice question.

A group of chess enthusiasts checked into a hotel &
were standing in the lobby discussing their recent
tournament victories. After about an hour, the
manager came out of his office & asked them to
disperse. "But why?" they asked. "Because", he
replied "I can't stand chess-nuts boasting in an open
foyer".

I just put a Christmas card through my neighbours
front door. It would have been so much easier if they
had a letterbox.

I got a Christmas card earlier and on the envelope it
said 'open with a smile'. It took me ages, I should
have just used my hands.

I've spent ages preparing the ingredients for the
Christmas cake and now they've ended up all over
the bottom of the oven. How the hell am I supposed
to put the dish in at 180 degrees?

Just plucked and stuffed the Turkey. Didn't have the
heart to kill it.

For Christmas my wife got me a weekend away in a hotel with my very own master-bedroom, which had its own fridge, double bed and minibar. How suite.

There are 364 days until Christmas, and people already have their Christmas lights up. (If read on Boxing Day).

If you were disappointed with what you received this Christmas, just remember somewhere, someone unwrapped an aston villa shirt.

I think I've been eating too much salmon over Christmas. I've just tried to run up an escalator that was going down.

The jumper I got for Christmas kept picking up static electricity so I took it back to the shop and exchanged it for another one free of charge.

My New Years resolution is to stop using aerosol deodorants. Roll on next year.

My New Years resolution is to see things through right until the e

A New Years resolution is something that goes in one year and out of the other.

My New Years resolution is to cover my whole house in Velcro, and I'm going to stick to it.

Bought the kids a trampoline for Xmas. Took it back today as it was useless. There was no bounce in it & the legs were facing the wrong way.

This year I thought I'd release a Christmas record called 'Duvet know it's Christmas?"
It's a cover version.

My son has asked for a train set for Christmas, but I can't find one, so I've bought him a replacement bus service set instead.

I asked the wife what she wanted for Christmas. She said, "Some chocolate and a nice surprise". Kinder egg it is then.

The coal industrys Christmas party was great, a real meeting of mines.

Why did the Scottish dwarf with a perm celebrate Christmas on the 18th December?
Because he was a wee curly.

It's still three months until Pancake Tuesday, but already the shops are full of flour, milk and eggs. How ridiculous!

To all those who received a book from me as a Christmas present. They are due back at the library today.

Health

I went to the doctors today with a hearing problem. He said "Can you describe the symptoms?" I said "Homer's a fat bloke and Marge has blue hair".

Please say a prayer for my mother in law. She's in hospital because a bee landed on her face. It didn't sting her though, I was just too quick with the spade.

Went to the doctors the other day and said "Do you treat alcoholics?" and the GP said, "Of course we do". So I said "Brilliant, fancy taking me to the pub then coz I'm skint?"

Man goes to the Doctor with a strawberry growing out of his head. Doc says "I'll give you some cream for that".

I've just got a doctors appointment about my constipation. Unfortunately I can't go.

"You don't look well at all", said my doctor as I walked into his office desk.

Yesterday, I was diagnosed as an idiot. I returned to the hospital today, believing my condition had improved, only to be told by the car park ticket machine that there was no change.

Bloke walked in to the doctors. Doctor said "Gout?" Bloke said "I've only just come in".

Drove to the hospital today and noticed a sign there 'car thieves operate here'. I think the recent cutbacks are going too far now.

Just got a letter back from my Doctor saying that my blood was a type oh. Must be a type O.

"Doctor, doctor, I can't stop singing the 'wheels on the bus' song". "Don't worry, there's something going round and round", he replied.

Man: "Doctor doctor, I feel like a cowboy". Doctor: "Really, how long have u felt like this for?" Man: "About a yeeeeeeeeaaaaarrrrrrrr".

Just had a medical at the doctors. He said "Don't eat anything fatty". I said "Like bacon and burgers?" He said "No fatty, don't eat anything".

I went to see my doctor the other day and he said I needed a pacemaker. Now I have a Kenyan in front of me everywhere I go.

Just been to the hospital to pick up an x-Ray. His name is Rachel now.

I had a neck brace fitted at the hospital six months ago. I've not looked back since.

I went to the doctors with a carrot sticking out of my ear. He said that I'm not eating properly.

I went to the doctors with jelly and cream in my left ear and custard and fruit in my right ear. He said I was a trifle deaf.

I'm in hospital at the moment having poisoned myself by eating a daffodil bulb thinking it was an onion bulb. The doctor says that I'm not to worry as I'll be out in the spring.

"Excuse me doctor, my husband was rushed in with violent spasms in his buttocks. Where is he?" "ICU baby, shaking that ass" he replied.

My neck was clicking so I went to the Doctors. He said "In seven days time, it will make a noise when it clicks"."So when should I come to see you again?" I asked."Neck Squeak" he replied.

A man walked into the doctors with a lettuce leaf sticking out of his ear. "That's strange" said the doctor. "That's just the tip of the iceberg" said the man.

My doctor has given me some anti-gloating cream. Now all I want to do is rub it in.

One of my legs is a lot longer than the other. I'm always thinking what's the best treatment, but I just keep going round in circles.

I said to my doctor, "I've got a problem with the hearing in one of my ears". He said, "Are you sure?" I said, "Yes, I'm definite".

My doctor has just informed me that my voicebox is damaged and I may never speak again. I can't tell you how upset I am.

Medical definitions :-
1. WOUND - trauma involving division of tissue or rupture of the integument or mucous membrane, due to external violence or some mechanical agency rather than disease.
2. INJURY - him that sang with the Blockheads.

Went back to the doctors this morning as the tablets he gave me a couple of days ago were making me veer to the left and then to the right. He told me not to worry as these were just the side effects.

Man goes to the doctor with heart problems. The doctor gives him a jar of pills and tells him to take a pill one day, then skip a day, then take another pill the next day, then skip a day, and so on until the jar is empty. Next week his wife came in to see the doc. "He died", she said. "The pills seemed to be OK, but it was the skipping that killed him".

A man came round in hospital after a serious accident. He shouted, "Doctor, I can't feel my legs" The Doctor replied, "I know, I've cut your arms off".

Just got back from Turkey. Saw a sign over there saying 'English speaking Doctors'. Now, wouldn't that be nice in this Country?

Went to the doctors this morning to see if he could do anything about all the spots that I've got. He gave me some ointment to rub in. "Will it work?" I asked him. Doctor replied, "I don't like to make rash promises".

A blonde went to the hospital to donate her blood. The nurse asked her "What type are you?" The blonde replied "I'm an outgoing cat lover".

I went to the doctors today, saying I kept seeing an insect spinning in front of my eyes. The doctor replied "Yes, there's a bug going round".

Went to the doctors this morning saying my mouth was smelly and felt prickly. He said I had hollytosis.

"Doctor, doctor - I keep making people think I'm about to tell them a joke".

Scientists have developed a laser procedure to remove haemorrhoids, so you could say, there is light at the end of the tunnel.

A man goes to the doctors because his eyes won't stop producing a yellow liquid. The doctor examines him and says, "Your left eye is producing excessive amounts of urine and so too is your right eye". The man replies, "Oh no, not another pee pee eye".

I went to the doctors yesterday and asked for a repeat prescription. He said, "prescription, prescription".

I tried making some of those 'Hand-made Kettle Chips' last night. My friend in A&E is typing this for me.

I was feeling pretty rundown the other day so rather than waste my doctors time, I went to the chemist, told him how I felt and asked him, "Can you make something up?" He thought for a moment and then said, "Rod Stewart was in here earlier".

I dropped a bottle of Omega 3 pills on my foot. Don't worry though, I only suffered super-fish-oil injuries.

I couldn't undo the buttons on my jumper so I tried pulling it over my head. Unfortunately it got stuck so I'm now in A&E waiting to see a cardyologist.

Celebrities

I asked Jonathon Ross what the currency was in India and he suddenly became very excited.

If John Lennon was still alive, he could have written a song about instant pay and receive money services. Imagine all the paypal.

John Lennon had a secret art collection, painted entirely in mauve, lilac, violet and lavender. Imagine all the purple.

Wouldn't it be amazing if John Lennon had invented that device people put in their front doors to see who is on the other side? Imagine all the peepholes.

William Tell asks his son, "Do you know anyone who is good at shooting arrows son?" His son replies, "Not off the top of my head".

A man dressed as a highwayman came up to me and said, "Stand and deliver". I said, "Are you certain about this?" "Absolutely", he replied, "I'm adamant".

This Wayne Rooney bloke is the sort that would stare at a bottle of orange juice because it says 'concentrate'.

Have you heard Neil Diamonds new Christmas song? I can't recall the lyrics but I remember it had a sweet carol line.

Dad: "Go to your room now!" Child: *storms off* "Jim Morrison was overrated!"
Dad: "What did I tell you about slamming The Doors?"

I had just hung up from my phone on the bus this morning when I got a tap on the shoulder. "Excuse me", said a teenage girl, "I wonder if you could settle an argument for us? Me and my friend overheard your phone ringing and I'm pretty sure it was Beyonce, but my friend said it was Rihanna". I said "Your both wrong, it was my mum".

The Proclaimers garden looks terrible and they've scoured Scotland in an attempt to find machinery to cut the long grass. To date it's Bathgate no mower, Linwood no mower, Irvine no mower.

Xfactor contestants are ruining Queen songs. Roger Taylor probably doesn't mind, but Brian May.

The bodies of an Elvis impersonator, a Tom Jones impersonator and a Kylie Minogue lookalike have been found in a hotel room in London. The police believe a copycat killer is on the loose.

I've decided to stop watching the TV programme Cheers for a couple of weeks and do something completely different. I'm taking a break from Norm.

For many years there was a bully in our workplace and I had to work alongside him.
But on the plus side, it was great to be working on the same show as Jim Bowen.

I really need to be more subtle next year regarding Christmas presents. I was hinting this year that I needed a Dell ... still, it's not a bad cd.

As I looked at the ABBA quiz leader board I noticed that I was joint bottom with a Japanese girl. She glanced at the leader board and said, "No win me, no win you".

Dr Dre has a new album out, which was recorded in the western region of the Czech Republic. It's called Bohemian Rap CD.

I once got so badly beaten by Robin, Doris and Darren, I didn't know what Day it was.

I've been diagnosed with a type of amnesia. I deny the existence of certain 80s bands. There is no cure.

Bono and The Edge walk into a bar. The barman says, "Oh no, not U2 again".

When I heard Stephen Hawking had reached 70, I thought, "Crikey, that's one powerful wheelchair".

Did anyone get that text going around? You've won £100 or tickets for an Elvis tribute concert. Press 1 for the money or 2 for the show.

Just taken my sat nav back. I got it with Bonnie Tyler's voice but it kept telling me to turn around and every now and then it fell apart.

Sean Connery thought he'd found a famous old racehorse down a cul-de-sac earlier. But later found out he was mistaken. He said, "It was close, but no Shergar".

Mesut Ozil was in the Gunners club shop. "Can I have a polo shirt, a pair of tracksuit bottoms, and a pair of trainers for my boss please?" he asked. "Sure", came the reply. "But why do you need all this stuff?" "Because my manager told me it's about time I got my Arsene gear".

Vincent Price is taller than Katie Price but not as heavy as Alan Price. I got this information from a Price comparison site.

Bonnie Tyler has released a cardiology DVD. It's totally clips of the heart.

I came home from the auction with a signed photograph of Ronnie Corbett whilst my brother bought a signed photograph of Ronnie Barker. So, it was a good buy from me and a good buy from him.

To get over my obsession, I threw away all the books I'd collected on Dusty Springfield. Now, I just don't know what to do with my shelf.

Money has gone missing from the Fleetwood Macs dressing room again. They're starting to suspect Stevie nicks.

Tesco have withdrawn its Simply Roast Meatloaf after finding it contained a Bat out of Hell.

Cindy Laupers roast lamb was horrible, I think she over-seasoned it with thyme after thyme.

The South African police have said that Oscar Pistorius may get the electric chair.
If you ask me he was dangerous enough on a pair of stilts, never mind giving him a mobility scooter.

After 39 years of allegations, Video is still fighting its case for killing the radio star.

I met Phil Spectors brother Crispin yesterday. He's head of quality control at Walkers.

Carol Vorderman fell down some stairs yesterday. On the way down she hit three from the top and two from the bottom.

My cat's a massive Paul Simon fan. You can call miaow.

Which cricket player is known for carrying around a broken zippo? Andrew Flintoff.

I rang an engineer earlier to say I was stuck in the lift and the music was driving me mad.
I think it was level 42.

I see they're bringing out a movie in commemoration of Eddie Stobart. I've just seen the trailer.

Have you had to walk 500 miles? Were you advised to walk 500 more? If so, you could be entitled to compensation. Call the Pro-Claimers now.

At any given time, the temptation to sing 'The lion sleeps tonight' is just a whim away.

The lead singer of that band in the joke above has died. He was eaten by a shark, he couldn't whim away.

I wonder if Hank Marvin gets fed every time he introduces himself.

I remember seeing Dr Hook in the 70's. Worst prostrate examination ever.

It was all go in the 60's and I was carried everywhere by Roy Wood. I was always on the Move.

Arrived home to find a pretty woman grouting the bathroom wall & singing 'It's a heartache'. I thought to myself, she's a bonny tiler.

Have you been hit by a rhythm stick? If so, you could be entitled to compensation for personal Ian Dury.

A bloke just came up to me whilst I was walking my Grandson. Looking down into the pram he said, "He's a bonny lad. What's his name?" "Andy Murray", I said. "Oh!" He laughed. "Because you think he's going to be good at tennis?" "No," I said, "Because he keeps losing his bottle".

Jonathan Ross has been accused of shoplifting a kitchen utensil from Tesco. Ross said it was a whisk he was prepared to take.

As the Beckhams welcome Harper Seven into the world, their day was tinged with sadness as it transpires there was a twin that died at birth. Tento Eight will be sorely missed.

I was at the Tate Modern Gallery with my friend today and we saw a painting of a man with frizzy hair which had the name 'Garfunkel' written underneath. My friend said, "I like it, but is it Art?"

I was in a restaurant last night when I asked the waiter if I could see the specials.
They were in the kitchen playing Ghost Town.

I was in a restaurant last night when I asked the waiter if I could see the specials.
"He replied, "Sorry, no specials, it's been madness today".

I was in a restaurant last night when I asked the waiter if I could see the specials. He replied, "Get lost, can't you see I'm busy, we have no specials today". Just bad manners I thought.

Last night I went out with Pamela Anderson. It was okay, but I would have preferred it without her son.

Just won second place in a Fidel Castro lookalike competition. Close, but no cigar.

Amazon have a decent deal on at the moment. If you buy any Adam & the Ants sheet music, they will throw in a free stand and deliver.

Went to bed last night thinking I was Peter Noone from Hermans Hermits. Woke up this morning feeling fine.

David Attenborough has been filming a rare large white wading bird in Africa.
Customs discovered the footage and arrested him for Storking.

I had a job cleaning a crime scene for a small pop star. I was dusting for Prince.

On his visit to Ireland the pope was asked what he thought of 'County Down?'
"It's not the same since Carol Vorderman left", he replied.

Jimmy Saville got stuck in a time-machine... now then, now then, now then...

My mates' wife has just left him because of his obsession with Fantasy Football, a bit harsh, but in his defence he has Smalling, Vertonghen, Monreal & Cahill.

My neighbour keeps banging on my wall when I'm playing my music, shouting "A little respect please". I shouted back, "I'm not an Erasure fan, but ok, this next one is for you".

My Employers offered me some DVDs today in lieu of profit sharing - Moonstruck, Witches of Eastwick, Silkwood, Mask. I don't like Cher options.

I was in the bank earlier. The woman behind the counter started singing "Downtown".
I thought to myself, "What a peculiar clerk".

I dj'd at my local pub last night. I played 'this old house', 'green door' and then 'you drive me crazy'. It got better after a shaky start.

Marvin Gaye used to keep a sheep in my grandfathers vineyard. He herd it on the grapevine.

Sean Connerys book case fell down earlier. He only has his shelf to blame.

If a bald fat guy collapses in the street and I suggest he's bust a blood vessel, would that be bad manners?

"Oh look, it's Ian McKellen, one of Britain's greatest actors", I said to my mates upon seeing him in my local pub. "Actually", he said "I'm Sir Ian". "My mistake", I apologised to my mates, "It's one of those refugees".

A spectator ran onto the track and punched Usain Bolt in the face. Police believe it to be race related.

'Benjamin Button'."BENJAMIN WHO?" "Benjamin" "WHO'S THERE?" 'Knock knock!'

My kids have been amazingly well behaved since we hired a native New Zealander to take care of them. He's a proper Maori Poppins.

My pet mouse Elvis died today. He was caught in a trap.

So William Shatner, the guy from Star Trek, decided to have a market for clothes. It was going pretty well until he decided to make pants.

Paul McCartney had to have a shave this morning. Yesterday, all his stubble seemed so far away.

I've just downloaded a Joe Hart screensaver on my computer. Now I can't save anything.

Roger Daltrey from The Who has installed wind turbines at his home. Now he just keeps talking about his generation.

When asked about his decision to why he resigned from his latest job as a football manager, Dick Advocaat replied, "I don't know, someone just poured lemonade over me and it snowballed from there".

Fred Flintstone took his car to the garage. "What seems to be the trouble?" asks the mechanic. "I think there's something wrong with my feet" replied Fred.

I've found a way to set my phone up so it plays 'Teenage Kicks' when anyone calls.
It's under 'tones'.

Just put my new jeans on and they started singing Waterloo Sunset. Apparently I have a kink in my trousers.

In case the country gets invaded and I have to quickly hide I have a big pop art painting on my wall that hides a secret panic room. I call it my handy war hole.

Felix Baumgartner. What a 'down to earth' chap.

I put some new body spray on last night, but I only managed to pull Anne Robinson. It must have been the weakest lynx.

It's a little known fact that Robert Mugabe is from Yorkshire. If you read his surname backwards, the clue is there.

Went in to the record shop today and asked if they had anything by The Doors. "Just fire extinguishers", they replied.

I think I just saw Michael J Fox in the florists. Not quite sure though as he had his back to the fuschias.

Neil Armstrong's initials are not applicable to me.

It's been seven hours and fifteen days since my wife left me due to my Sinead O'Connor obsession.

Every time I see Sacha Baron Cohen on television, I come out in a rash. I must have an Ali G.

Shania Twain has given birth to a baby boy. Choo Choo weighed in at 6lb 8oz.

Just got back from the video shop. I asked to borrow 'Batman Forever' but they said "No, I'd have to take it back tomorrow".

Police are treating Joe Fraziers death as suspicious. They're grilling George Foreman.

Jimmy Saville, Rolf Harris and Stuart Hall walk in to an Irish bar. The landlord says, "Not yew tree again?"

An asteroid has narrowly missed earth by 201,000 miles. Scientists have named it Emily Heskey.

In the last 15 years we have lost Johnny Cash, Steve Jobs, Bob Hope and Jimmy Saville, so now we have no cash, no jobs, no hope and no-one to fix it.

Mcbusted – sounds like somebody getting caught stealing a happy meal.

"No, you can't wear your 'Star Wars' mask when we go out tonight", said my wife.
"So you can just take that Luke off your face", she added.

I've just bought a U2 Satnav but had to take it back. The streets have no name and I still haven't found what I'm looking for.

My mate used to brag relentlessly whenever he recognised a song from the 90s quicker than me. Then, one day, I beat him to a Pulp.

I used to be in a Goth rock band called Prevention. We were better than The Cure.

Thought I saw Van Morrison in my rear view mirror the other day until I realised that everything in a mirror is reversed. Turned out to be a Morrisons van.

Downloaded a game based on 1980's British Funk. I can't get past Level 42.

The Irish

Bloke at the races whispers to Paddy "Do you want the winner of the next race?" Paddy replies "No thanks, I've only got a small garden".

Mick walks into Paddys barn and catches him dancing naked and playing with himself in front of a tractor. Mick says, "Oh, no, Paddy, what ya doing?" Paddy says, "Well me and Mary haven't been getting on in the bedroom lately & the therapist recommended I do something sexy to attracter".

Paddy says to Mick, "Christmas is on a Friday this year". Mick says "Let's hope it's not the 13th".

The plumber said, "Paddy, why haven't you paid my bill yet for the work I did last Friday?"
Paddy replied, "Well it wasn't what you quoted". "I didn't give you a quote", said the plumber. Paddy replied, "When I asked what day could you come, you said you were free Friday".

Paddy applied for a job to be a blacksmith. The blacksmith asks "Have you ever shoed a horse?" Paddy replies, "No, but I once told a donkey off".

My mate Paddy just told me that he robbed a shop last night. "What did you get?" I asked. "26 pictures", he smiled, showing me, "The cheapest one is worth over £180,000". I said, "Pad, these are from an estate agents".

Paddy buys a bath but takes it back the next day complaining that the water keeps running out. "Did you buy a plug?" asks the salesman. "I didn't realise it was electric" replied Paddy.

Two Irish men sitting in a pub. The landlord came over and said "You can't eat your own food in here". So they swapped sandwiches.

Paddy's in the shower and Murphy shouts "Did you find the shampoo?" Paddy shouts back "Yes, but it's for dry hair and I've just wet mine".

Paddy is on his First Aid course when the question came up "What would you do if your child swallowed the front door key?" Paddy responded with "I'd go in through the window".

"Tree across the track near the level crossing" said Paddy's missus as she was checking her Facebook newsfeed, "And two down on the road near the swan pub".
"You know I'm thick" shouted Paddy "Stop asking me stupid crossword questions".

Paddy took two tatty stuffed dogs to the Antiques Roadshow. The presenter said they were very rare as they were produced by the best taxidermist before the turn of the century. "Any idea what they would fetch if they were in good condition ?" asked the presenter. "Sticks" replied Paddy.

Ryanair pilot Paddy is about to land his plane when a problem develops so he calls the tower and says "Help, help, Easter, Pancake Tuesday, New Years Eve, Bank holiday Monday, Bonfire Night, Christmas, Shrove Tuesday!!!!!!! Voice comes back and says " For crying out loud Paddy, it's Mayday".

A Muslim was sitting next to Paddy on a plane. Paddy ordered a whisky. The stewardess asked the Muslim if he'd like a drink. He replied in disgust "I'd rather be raped by a dozen whores than let liquor touch my lips". Paddy handed his drink back and said "Me too, I didn't know we had a choice".

Paddy calls Ryanair to book a flight. The operator asks "How many people are flying with you?" Paddy replies "I don't know, It's your bloody plane".

Paddy and Murphy are working on a building site. Paddy says to Murphy "I'm gonna have the day off. I'm gonna pretend I'm mad" He climbs up the rafters, hangs upside down and shouts "I'M A LIGHT BULB! I'M A LIGHT BULB!" Murphy watches in amazement. The Foreman shouts "Paddy you're mad, go home" So he leaves the site. Murphy starts packing his kit up to leave as well. "Where the hell are you going?" asks the Foreman. "I can't work in the friggin' dark" says Murphy.

Paddy takes his new wife to bed on their wedding night. She undresses, lies on the bed spread-eagled and says "You know what I want, don't you?" "Yeah," says Paddy. "The whole bloody bed by the looks of it".

Michael O'Leary (the owner of the renown airline company that offers cheap flights until you come to add on all the "extras") walks in to a Dublin bar and orders a guiness. The bartender informs him it will be two Euros. Mr O'Leary says, "Be Jesus, that'll be a fine price will that" of which the bartender asks "Will you be wanting a glass with that?"

Paddy spies a letter lying on his doormat. It says on the envelope 'DO NOT BEND'.
Paddy spends the next 2 hours trying to figure out how to pick the thing up.

Paddy climbs up to the top board of the swimming baths with a large fish under his arm. Murphy shouts up, "What you gonna do with that?" Paddy replies, "Triple somersault with pike."

Paddy & Mick were talking, Paddy says "Mick, is there a B&Q in Leeds?" Mick says, "No, but I think there are 2 e's".

Irish police have just arrested a serial killer. He slashed 25 boxes of corn flakes before he was caught.

"Sorry Paddy, you can't come in to the pub dressed like that" said the Landlord. "Why not?" asked Paddy. "Because you're wearing speedos" explained the landlord. "But I'm here for the pool competition" exclaimed Paddy.

Ryanair have gone too far this time. On the way home last night, my wife started crying at the book she was reading. Ryanair charged me £60 for emotional baggage.

Paddys' wife was about to give birth. The midwife asked, "How dilated is she?" "Bejaysus" he exclaimed. "We're both over the moon".

Paddys' wife told him he should put a pair of clean socks on every day. By Friday he couldn't get his boots on.

Met a bloke today called Toby Shaw, surprisingly he wasn't Irish.

Due to a water shortage in Ireland, Dublin swimming baths have announced they are closing lanes 7 and 8, after the original plan to dilute the water didn't work.

In Ireland today, a Cork man was found floating in the sea.

A family of Irish people were found dead outside the cinema over Christmas. Apparently they had frozen to death waiting to see 'Closed for Winter'.

On his death bed, Paddy says to Murphy, "When I die Murph, will you be pouring whisky over me body?" "That I will" replies Murphy, "But do you mind if it goes through me kidneys first?"

Adult

Jonathan Ross can fit two whole chocolate bars up his ar5e. He calls it his party Twix.

What's all the fuss about Christmas? Every day is like Christmas to me. I sit down to dinner every day with a fat bird who doesn't gobble any more.

Teacher asks the class, "Does anyone know the name of Robin Hoods girlfriend?"
Little Paddy puts his hand in the air and answers, "Trudy Glen". The teacher replies, "No Paddy, it's Maid Marion"."But the song goes Robin Hood, Robin Hood riding Trudy Glen", explains Paddy.

"Are you sure you want this?" I asked my wife. "When I'm done, you won't be able to sit down for weeks". She nodded. "Okay", I said, putting the three-piece suite on eBay.

"Are you sure you can take the pain?" she demanded, brandishing stilettos.
"I think so", I gulped. "Here we go then", she said, and showed me the receipt.

Bought some rohypnol the other day and on the back it said "best before date".

An elderly couple, who were both widowed, had been going out with each other for a long time. Urged on by their friends, they decided it was finally time to get married. Before the wedding, they went out to dinner and had a long conversation regarding how their marriage might work. They discussed finances, living arrangements and so on. Finally, the old gentleman decided it was time to broach the subject of their physical relationship. "How do you feel about sex?" he asked, rather tentatively. "I would like it infrequently" she replied.
The old gentleman sat quietly for a moment, adjusted his glasses, leaned over towards her and whispered, "Is that one word or two?"

"It's a boy!" I shouted tears rolling down my face "I don't believe it. A boy!"
It was at that moment I decided I'd never visit Thailand again.

A pretty young gypsy girl knocked on my door and asked if I had any old clothing. I said, " Yes, but what would I get in return?" She said I could play with her breasts. I thought, "That's fair, tit for tat".

I was offered sex with a 21 year old girl today. In exchange, I was supposed to advertise some kind of bathroom cleaner. Of course I declined, because I am a person with high moral standards and strong willpower. Just as strong as Ajax, the super strong bathroom cleaner. Now available with scented lemon or vanilla.

My Mrs asked me to get one of those penis enlargers, so I did. She's 22 and her name's Lucy.

How come you can get the Steve Irwin biography on DVD but not on Blue Ray?

The latest bra for middle-aged women is called the "Sheep Dog". It rounds them up & points them in the right direction.

I googled 'Gary Oldman' and got some pretty disturbing images. He's really let himself go I thought. Then I realised I'd left the "r" out.

"Where's all this shit coming from?" thought the fan.

"Breaking News" The inventor of the Anagram has died today. May he "erect a penis".

A human fart can be louder than a trombone. I discovered this at my daughters' school concert.

One day a father gets out of work and on his way home he suddenly remembers that it's his daughters birthday. He pulls over to a toy shop and asks the sales person, "How much for one of those Barbies in the display window?" The salesperson answers, "Which one do you mean, Sir? We have Work Out Barbie for £19.95, Shopping Barbie for £19.95, Beach Barbie for £19.95, Disco Barbie for £19.95, Ballerina Barbie for £19.95, Astronaut Barbie for £19.95, Skater Barbie for £19.95, and Divorced Barbie for £265.95". The amazed father asks, "It's what? Why is the Divorced Barbie £265.95 and the others only £19.95?"
The annoyed salesperson rolls her eyes, sighs, and answers, "Sir, Divorced Barbie comes with: Kens Car, Kens House, Kens Boat, Kens Furniture, Kens Computer, one of Kens Friends, and a key chain made with Kens balls".

Sex is a lot like quantum physics. I've heard of it.

A man in the street asked me for a sperm sample to fertilise a chimpanzee's ovaries, so I punched him in the face. No-one makes a monkey out of me.

This German shepherd craps on my lawn each morning. Today, he even brought his dog.

My wife keeps calling me a hypochondriac. It's like she doesn't even care I've sprained my uterus.

Was talking to a young guy last night who wanted to be a teacher in an orphanage. I thought how recommendable until I realised he just didn't like parent evenings.

Brought the Xmas tree today. The assistant said "Putting it up yourself?" I replied, "No, in the living room".

So, I just got stopped by the Police as part of their "Christmas Drink-Driving Campaign"
The female copper asks me, "How many drinks have you had in the last 24 hours?"
Apparently, "Not enough to shag you!" was the wrong answer. I need a lift back from custody.

I heard some sad news today. After seven years of medical training and hard work, my very good friend has been struck off after one minor indiscretion and I think it's outrageous . He slept with one of his patients and now can no longer work in the profession that he loves. What a waste of time, training and money. A genuinely nice guy and a brilliant vet.

I got a new stick deodorant today. The instructions said, "Remove cap and push up bottom". I can barely walk, but whenever I fart the room smells lovely.

Why is Viagra like insomnia? They both keep you up all night.

You really do have to feel sorry for all those Villa fans travelling home. Aston is a f***ing shit hole.

Just bought cluedo, swingers edition. Turns out they all did it ... in every room.

Just had a letter back from Screwfix Direct thanking me for my interest but they are not a dating agency.

After years of teasing my girlfriend about her anorexia, she finally snapped.

A chauffer is driving his rich lady to the shops when he gets a puncture. He gets out and with a lot of effort, tries to get the wheel hobs off. After 10 minutes he's still struggling so the lady says "Do you want a screwdriver?" Of which he replied, "We might as well as I can't get these bloody hubs off".

"If you'd had a tin of shoe polish, you could have blackened her up and got away with it," I said to Oscar Pistorius, laughing. Then I realised that was in bad taste. Why would he have a tin of shoe polish?

My dad has a manicure set. The other day, he asked me if I wanted to use his 'male grooming kit'. I replied, "What do you think I am, a Catholic priest?"

Took a girl who was suffering with rickets home with me last night. Cracking legs.

Is it true that the Samaritans are about to open a new drop-in centre at Beachy Head?

I've got a book coming out soon - shouldn't have eaten it really.

I've got viagraphobia. It makes me scared stiff.

Disabled puppet looking for casual sex, no strings attached.

I saw a guy stacking shelves at Tesco today, complaining that the top shelf was broken. He had a wrecked aisle defunction.

I met a 14 year old girl on the internet. She was clever, funny, flirty and sexy, so I suggested we meet up. She turned out to be an undercover detective. How cool is that at her age?

Vicar booking into a hotel asks the receptionist "Is the Porn channel in my room disabled?" "No" she replies "It's just regular porn you sick *******".

A guy walks in to the psychiatrist wearing only cling film for shorts. The shrink says, "Well, I can clearly see you're nuts."

Guy walks into the Doctors with a steering wheel down his pants, "You've got to help me Doc, it's driving me nuts".

A seal walks in to a club………

Last night I reached for my liquid Viagra and accidentally swigged from a bottle of Tippex. I woke up this morning with a huge correction.

I tried an old Viagra pill last night that I found at the back of the bathroom cupboard. It didn't work. I think it was passed its swell by date.

I take half a Viagra a day. It stops me pissing on my slippers.

Just spent over an hour at the doctors' because of strange voices coming from my pants, and all he said was "Ignore them, they're talking bollocks".

When I was a kid we used to play football on a piece of grass near a bridge where a lot of people committed suicide. We used the jumpers as posts.

I'm in a band called Dyslexic. We've just released our greatest shit album.

Claims that there was a cure for dyslexia was like music to my arse.

LEROY'S HEARING

In a Tottenham church Sunday morning a preacher said, "Anyone with 'special needs' who wants to be prayed over, please come forward to the front of the altar". With that, Leroy got in line and when it was his turn the Preacher asked, "Leroy, what do you want me to pray about for you?" Leroy replied, "Preacher, I need you to pray for help with my hearing".

The preacher put one finger of one hand in Leroy's ear, placed his other hand on top of Leroy's head, and then prayed and prayed and the whole congregation joined in with much enthusiasm. After a few minutes, the preacher removed his hands, stood back and asked, "Leroy how is your hearing now?"

Leroy answered, "I don't know. It ain't 'til Thursday".

I stole my girlfriends wheelchair. I knew she'd come crawling back to me.

"Dad...I've been watching that shaky person from next door trying to get his car into the garage for the last 20 minutes". "Your Mum will tell you that's parking son".

Women always say that giving birth is way more painful than a guy getting kicked in the nuts. Here is proof that they are wrong. A year or so after giving birth, a woman will often say "It'd be nice to have another baby". You never hear a bloke say "I wouldn't mind another kick in the nuts". Case closed.

The new reproductive exhibit at the London Zoo Reptile House has been temporarily closed because of a reptile dysfunction.

Better to be pissed off than pissed on.

I left a trail of rose petals from the front door, up the stairs and in to the bedroom. I sprinkled some more over the bed. I put a bottle of prosecco in to a cooler and left it on the bedside table with two glasses. I sat in the corner of the room wearing nothing but a silk gown. I wanted this to be the best romantic night ever and was getting nervous when I heard her key in the front door and then her walking up the stairs. Now all I needed was a perfect way to introduce myself.

On his 70th birthday, a man was given a gift certificate from his wife. The certificate was for consultation with an Indian medicine man living on a nearby reservation who was rumoured to have a simple cure for erectile dysfunction. The husband went to the reservation and saw the medicine man. The old Indian gave him a potion and with a grip on his shoulder warned, '"This is a powerful medicine. You take only a teaspoonful, and then say '1-2-3.' When you do, you will become more manly than you have ever been in your life, and you can perform for as long as you want". The man thanked the old Indian and as he walked away, he turned and asked, "How do I stop the medicine from working?" "Your partner must say '1-2-3-4'" he responded, "but when she does, the medicine will not work again until the next full moon". He was very eager to see if it worked so he went home, showered, shaved, took a spoonful of the medicine, and then invited his wife to join him in the bedroom. When she came in, he took off his clothes and said, "1-2-3". Immediately, he was the manliest of men. His wife was excited and began throwing off her clothes, and then she asked, "What was the 1-2-3 for?"

They say that sex is the best form of exercise. Now correct me if I'm wrong but I don't think 2 minutes and 15 seconds every 6 months is going to shift this beer belly.

A woman has sued a hospital stating that after recent treatment her husband had lost interest in sex. The doctors replied: 'All we did was correct his eye sight'.

Picked this girl up last night in the local bar. She asked if we could make out. I said "My van is round the corner, we can go in the back of that if you like". She agreed but just before we climbed in, she said "I'm a bit kinky, do you mind if I whip you whilst we are making out?" I didn't mind, but not having anything in the van, I snapped off my aerial and passed it to her. After 30 minutes of heightened pleasure, I dropped her off home, but my chest, back & legs were cut to ribbons, seeping blood and really painful. The next morning, it was still very painful, so I decided to see my doctor. I explained what happened so he said, "Better take a look, take your clothes off". After a quick examination he said, "Good gracious, that's the worst case of van aerial disease I've ever seen".

23654021R00130

Printed in Poland
by Amazon Fulfillment
Poland Sp. z o.o., Wrocław